BROWN'S LAWSUIT COOKBOOK

BY MICHAEL H. BROWN

Desert Publications
El Dorado, AR 71731-1751 U. S. A.

Brown's Lawsuit Cookbook

by

Michael H. Brown

Desert Publications
P.O. Box 1751
El Dorado, AR 71731-1751
501-862-2077

ISBN 0-87947-367-3
12 11 10 9 8 7 6
Printed in U. S. A.

Desert Publication is a division of
The DELTA GROUP, Ltd.
Direct all inquires & orders to the above address.

Table of Contents

INTRODUCTION

This is probably the first "how to be your own lawyer" book ever written by a non-lawyer. There are two good reasons for this.

The first is that if any members of the Bar Association divulged the information I am about to, he would be disbarred immediately, tarred, feathered, and run out of town on a rail. For openers.

The second is that every scrap of information I put in front of you is real. It works. I learned every bit of it the hard way, starting on September 10, 1974, when the FBI arrested me and sent me to prison for 3½ years - where I learned "jailhouse law" - up until this book was written. During that time, I have won a number of cases, both in federal and state court.

I lost some, too.

You'll understand why I lost the ones I did by the time you finish reading this book. Most of the ones I lost had absolutely nothing to do with the facts or the controlling principles of law on the case.

Michael H. Brown
Berea, Kentucky
November 4, 1980

1. How To Use This Book

This is a how-to-do-it book. It simply covers the mechanics of how to sue someone else and, hopefully, win. It is not a philosophical treatise on "what's wrong with the system" or a collection of pre-printed forms on filling out a will, filing for divorce, etc. Every case in this book can be verified by actual court records, with two exceptions. On the first case, the names and the docket number of the case have been changed to protect the guilty. He wasn't really that bad a guy and I don't feel it necessary to ridicule him publicly. The last case in the book is a textbook example of how to stop forced bussing. I can't file it simply because my children are in no danger of being bussed in rural Kentucky—the courts don't accept claims, petitions, or writs merely for the sake of academic exercise.

The first thing that you must overcome to use this manual effectively is an "awe of the law"—the statutes, lawyers, and judges themselves. If you are easily intimidated or—in prison jargon—a "trembler", you had better hang it up right at this point.

If, on the other hand, you're one of the enraged few who has "had it" with law and lawyers, read on. You may find some real eye-openers.

The second thing that you must overcome to use this manual effectively is a programmed ignorance being no fault of your own but rather a series of myths perpetuated by those in whose interest the status quo lies.

The legal profession.

At one time, this nation had three branches of government.

The executive. The legislative. The judicial.

Now, we have only one. The lawyers.

Let me give you just one specific example of the type of incestuous relationships they create and how it affects the rest of us.

A fellow named S. Hugh Dillin ran for governor of Indiana some years back. The voters rejected him, saying, in effect, they did not want him ruling over them. So he retired and never bothered the people of Indiana again, right?

Wrong.

At least if he had been elected and misbehaved, the voters could have thrown him out on his ear at the end of his first term.

What happened was Dillin's fellow lawyers and political cronies got him appointed as a federal judge for the Southern District of Indiana. The reason I use him as an example, while there are hundreds of similar ones, is that he was the first federal judge I ever bested on an appeal. His judgment on the case was so asinine that even the Seventh Circuit Court of Appeals commented on it. This case is known in the law books as *Cox* v. *Benson*, 548 F 2nd 186. In a later chapter, I will show you how to read, understand, and reference law books.

Dillin is still on the federal bench. Since federal judges are appointed for life there is simply no way to get rid of him. Almost.

What the three branches of government being controlled by lawyers means to anyone trying to buck the government is that they are not dealing with law, but with lawyers.

Which means personalities.

And the higher you go, the more obvious it becomes.

Probably the most obvious example is Chief Justice Warren E. Burger's statement, quoted in THE BRETHREN, "We're the Supreme Court and we can do what we want!"

Nor is this a "new" way of doing anything.

In the 1930's, F.D.R. tried to "pack" the Supreme Court with men of his own choosing, making it self-evident that the "law of the land" depended not a whit upon justice but simply upon the personalities of the men sitting on the bench.

Richard Nixon was somewhat more successful. In some ways, today's Supreme Court could be referred to as "Nixon's Revenge".

This business of judgment by personality extends all the way down through the federal system and into some of the states. What I hope to do is teach you how to cope with it.

In all fairness, there are some decent judges. Primarily at the state level. There's a good reason for this. Here in Kentucky judges are elected to office. Further, it is a non-partisan office. That is, no political party can profit by putting "their man" in office and the judge can be tossed out if he misbehaves. The first time I appeared in a civil action in Kentucky, I was flabbergasted — the judge did absolutely everything according to the rules. In federal court, a non-lawyer fighting his own case is normally treated and looked upon as a species of life somewhat lower than a cockroach.

The federal system is a classic example of "how not to do things". Federal judges are appointed for life, supposedly in order to keep them from bowing to political pressures, to preserve the intergrity of the judiciary, to keep them free from corruption, etc.

Unfortunately, such a program has exactly the opposite effect.

What happens is that federal judges inhabiting a position that it takes a satchel of dynamite to dislodge them from can become unbelievably arrogant and totally, totally irresponsible. You'll learn more — and how to cope with them — later in this book.

Ironically, at the very moment I was writing these lines, my secretary came in with my November 10, 1980 (vol. 3—no. 9) copy of the National Law Journal. On the cover is an article about a federal judge in Cleveland named Frank Battisti who is busily—at the moment—cramming forced bussing down everyone's throats. His is a classic case of rule by lawyers (and it's typical):

Appointed to the bench by President Kennedy (a member of the Executive branch of government).

Mandated forced bussing on Cleveland citizens (a legislative function, forced bussing was *never* a law passed by Congress).

Took over the Cleveland school board (an executive function at the *state* level).

Federal judges arrogating power to themselves the Constitution or the Congress never intended has been fairly common since Andrew Jackson's term in office. It should be obvious to a child that the only way to stop this nonsense is to make a federal judgeship an elective office, the way we do it with state judgeships here in Kentucky. Of course, that would leave the political parties nowhere to dump their political and legal dinosuars.

Which brings us back to the legal dinosaurs.

The lawyers.

To do battle with an opposing side on a lawsuit—and the lawyer or lawyers on it—keep one further thing in mind.

Law is not a discipline like chemistry or physics. It does not require the years of training that, for example, a good machinist or mechanic must have.

It is merely a collection of indexed paragraphs, just like you would find in a comprehensive set of encyclopedias, written in plain English, and presided over by personalities (judges) and men who have an incredibly exaggerated opinion of their own intelligence (lawyers).

All that is actually necessary for the practice of law is a good grasp of English and the instruction necessary to use the indexing system to find what you want.

English comprehension you should have learned in high school.

This book will teach you the indexing system. And a lot more.

2. How To Sue

There are two basic types of court action in this country—civil and criminal. You can't file a criminal complaint, only a D.A. or a United States Attorney can. You can ask the D.A. to file one for you. Even if he does, the complaint still has to go to a grand jury—23 people—before an indictment can be handed down. This is true of both federal and state juries. The actual function of the grand jury is to investigate the investigators (really, why DO these government employees want to put this man in prison?) But that function has been diluted almost to the point of non-existence by prosecutorial misconduct over the past several decades.

Better you should file a civil action instead.

A civil action—or lawsuit—or tort— is merely a legal duel between opposing sides or individuals. Instead of drawing blood the winner gets cash. For an emotionally satisfying "win" you don't even have to get the money. Merely crippling the other side financially through legal fees is sometimes even better than stabbing or shooting. It is often easier (and cheaper) to recover from physical violence than it is a $12,000 attorney's bill.

Let's say, for example, someone shoots your dog with a pellet pistol. Your first instinct is to run over and punch him in the nose. However, that becomes assault and battery in most states and might land you in jail. Worse, he might whip your butt. Humiliating.

Take the military approach.

Hit him where a) he is weakest and b) there is the least chance that he can do you damage in return.

Sue.

A sample complaint for someone shooting your dog will look something like the example on the next two pages.

SAMPLE DOCUMENT

MADISON DISTRICT COURT

John Smith, Plaintiff	*		
v	*	Civil Action No. _______	
Joe Jones, Defendant	*		
	*		

JURISDICTION

1. Jurisdiction of this Court is invoked under K.R.S. 452.460(1).

PARTIES

2. Plaintiff has and has had a legal residence of 123 Holly Hill, Waco, Kentucky since March, 1972.

3. Defendant Jones moved into the adjoining residence October 1978 and is employed as the daytime manager of Baker's IGA, Waco.

FACTS

4. Plaintiff is the owner of one (1) AKC registered White German Shepherd puppy, approximately seven (7) months old.

5. Plaintiff previously owned another White German Shepherd purchased in 1970 which died of natural causes in late 1977.

6. Plaintiff has never had any previous complaints about the behavior of his dog(s) from anyone in the neighborhood, including the defendant.

SAMPLE DOCUMENT

7. At approximately 3 p.m. November 2, 1978 defendant Jones discharged a pellet pistol at plaintiff's German Shepherd, causing said animal copious bleeding after the projectile penetrated its right flank.

8. Plaintiff's German Shepherd was in the plaintiff's back yard.

LEGAL CLAIMS

9. The actions of the defendant were/are a violation of law under K.R.S. 84.220(10) and 258.245(1), but not limited thereto.

10. The defendant has no legal right whatsoever to:

A. Discharge a weapon into plaintiff's back yard.

B. Use plaintiff's German Shepherd for target practice.

C. Play "big game hunter" with plaintiff's property.

RELIEF REQUESTED

1. Plaintiff's cost of this action.

2. Trial by jury on all issues triable by jury.

3. Damages in the amount of $300.00 compensatory and $1200.00 punitive.

Notary Public:

June 14, 1980

Respectfully Submitted,

John Smith
123 Holly Hill
Waco, Kentucky 40446

The heading is merely the court that it belongs in. You can always find this out merely by calling the court clerk for the county you live in. However, you cannot always file the action in the same county you reside in. Here in Kentucky if the defendant lives in another county then you must file the complaint in that county. "Madison" in the preceeding is the county and "District Court" is simply one step up from small claims court in which matters involving less than $1,500 are contested. In Kentucky, simply phone the court clerk in the county courthouse to find out which court to file in — small claims, district, circuit, etc.

The plaintiff is the one filing the complaint.

The defendant is just what you think he would be: in this case the fellow who shot the dog. The plaintiff is always listed first, the defendant second, and each are so labeled.

The asterisks merely let the court clerk know at a glance that a lawsuit is concerned. The clerk is the one who gives it a docket number, filled in the blank behind Civil Action No. 79-C-592.

All 79-C-592 means is that the case was filed in 1979, it is a civil action (Cr is for criminal), and it is the 592nd case that was filed that year.

Jurisdiction is the court's authority to arbitrate or preside over the dispute. Look in the index under "jurisdiction" in any set of law books that has all the state laws in them (found in almost any public library) and you will find a statute or series of statutes authorizing you to file your action according to court.

In this case, K.R.S. 452.460(1) simply means Kentucky Revised Statutes, 452.460(1) tells you—in paragraph (1) — that you must file the lawsuit in the county the defendant resides in. The numbers to the right of the decimal point are merely a convenient way of allowing the state legislature to sandwich extra laws in between existing ones. They could just as easily have used letters. In some cases—such as in the federal system—letters and numbers are mixed together. More on that later.

The parties are the contestants. Plaintiff is again listed first. Where the parties live must be given. Otherwise it becomes impossible for the court to keep track of them.

You may have noticed by now that each paragraph is numbered. Normally it's not a "must" but it will help you keep track of everything later on.

The facts are what actually happened. As you may gather from paragraph seven there may be some exaggeration in the complaint. Sounds good, though, doesn't it?

The legal claims simply describe what wrongs you think that the defendant committed and what your basis is for that belief. This also constitutes claims for the judge and jury to chew on. Obviously you have no legal claim if your neighbor is merely ugly as a toad and you don't like looking at him.

In this case, the legal claims in paragraph 9 were arrived at simply by looking in the K.R.S. index under "cruelty to animals". A criminal complaint could have been filed also, though in most states this is a waste of time. Besides, you lose control of most of the situation.

Paragraph 10 merely contains claims in equity (fairness, law, justice).

In other cases, such behavior has become so commonplace that there are well-established guidelines for the "tort" (or civil wrong).

For example, if a mechanic told you that you needed a lot of work done on your car (that it didn't need), you paid to have it done (and even if he did it), that would be listed under "legal claims" as constituting the elements of the tort known as deceit:

1. A false representation made by the defendant. In the ordinary case, this representation must be one of fact.

2. Knowledge or belief on the part of the defendant that the representation is false—or, what is regarded as equivalent, that he has not a sufficient basis of information to make it. This element often is given the technical name of "scienter".

3. An intention to induce the plaintiff to act or to refrain from action in reliance upon the misrepresentation.

4. Justifiable reliance upon the representation on the part of the plaintiff, in taking action or refraining from it.

5. Damage to the plaintiff, resulting from such reliance.

Where these "elements" of torts are found is in a 1200+ page book titled Prosser's LAW OF TORTS put out by West

He wanted a refund, but wound up with apartment complex

SACRAMENTO, Calif. (AP) — All Terry Sundkvist wanted was his $50 cleaning deposit refunded. Now he "owns" the $1.5 million apartment complex where he once lived.

Using his knowledge of small claims court and a corporation's unwitting cooperation, the attorney was able to pay $449.31 at a county marshal's auction and receive a certificate of sale for the 95-unit Laura Dawn Manor.

The former owners, Sacland Investors, are trying to settle with Sundkvist so they can sell the complex. Sundkvist, now an attorney in Portland, Ore., says he has refused an offer of $10,000.

The firm also is disputing his claim in Sacramento Superior Court, calling the acquisition an "extraordinary windfall."

It all began in 1973, when the then 23-year-old McGeorge Law School student and his wife moved from their apartment.

Sundkvist says that when the manager said the cleaning deposit would not be returned although the apartment had been left clean, he wrote to the firm's legal agent, Patricia Lapan of San Leandro.

He says he received no reply. She claims she vaguely remembers instructing the manager he was not entitled to a refund.

On March 13, 1975, Sundkvist filed suit in small claims court, seeking $50 plus costs and $200 in punitive damages.

Mrs. Lapan was served with a summons May 4, 1976, but she ignored it, and on June 1, 1976, a default judgment of $312 was awarded to Sundkvist.

When he could not get Sacland to pay the judgment, Sundkvist requested that the county marshal's office auction off the complex to meet the court's judgment.

The sale was scheduled for Sept. 17, 1976, at the county courthouse and notices were sent to the parties involved. Only Sundkvist showed up and he was advised by marshals to bid for the property at $449.31, the amount of his judgment plus marshal's fees and interest. He got a certificate of sale of real estate.

Sacland had a year to pay the judgment and redeem title to the property, but the notice of the marshal's sale was returned unopened.

But Sacland took notice in August 1977, when it attempted to sell the property for $1.5 million and a title search turned up Sundkvist's claim.

Mrs. Lapan and the firm's other lawyers first offered Sundkvist $1,000 to clear the title, but Sundkvist ignored the letters until the time for redemption ran out.

The firm's lawyers offered Sundkvist more money to extend the redemption period, but his Sacramento lawyer, Clarence Brown, told them, "You're too late."

"Anyone could have done the same thing," Sundkvist said.

Publishing Co., P.O. Box 3526, St. Paul, Minnesota 55165. They do NOT like selling their books to non-lawyers. Gives the game away.

Other, more specialized tort elements, such as copyright violations must be found in more specialized books.

The "Relief Requested" is what you want the court to do about the situation. In this case, the plaintiff is asking for a trial by jury on the facts, (juries try the facts, judges explain the law to the jury and determine what the law is—except in federal courts, where judges often act as judge, jury, prosecutor, Congress, or whatever else they feel like), his cost of filing and prosecuting the lawsuit, and money damages.

Obviously, if he loses he doesn't get any of it.

The damages sued for simply mean compensatory, to compensate him for damage to his animal, and punitive, to punish the defendant and give him a disincentive to do it again.

The notary public merely attests to whose signature is on the lawsuit, not to the veracity of the statements themselves.

After the lawsuit has been typed up and notarized it has to be delivered to the defendant. Normally it can be done one of two ways: certified mail or by marshal. You can't file suit against someone and then not let him know about it, though in some cases some defendants (or their lawyers) are so unconscious, they never make a move until it's too late anyway. Get a load of the case on the opposite page.

I prefer paying a little extra to have live people serve the papers. Shakes the victim up. Especially if uniformed men with guns walk in where the guy works and hand him a legal paper. Gets all sorts of gossip started. All the defendant actually gets handed is a photocopy or carbon copy of the complaint.

The court clerk in your county will tell you exactly what you have to do to file the lawsuit (usually furnishing her with a certain number of copies and paying a filing fee, normally less than $100.00) and have marshals serve the papers. In the federal courts, a "marshal's service form" is used to charge you the service fee, mileage, etc. These are obtained from the marshal's office, not the clerk.

After the complaint has been filed and served the battle has just begun. Sometimes you get some unexpected fallout—like when the guy's wife sees his name in the newspaper as the one being sued, hits the roof, and leaves for days. All lawsuits in this country are considered public record and they WILL be published in the newspaper. If you're leaving the state and sue the poor slob for child molesting or other deviant behavior imagine the humiliation THAT would cause!

When the average mark gets hit with a lawsuit the first thing he does is run to his lawyer—and in many cases does more harm than good.

Get a load of this and then watch how it develops:

SAMPLE DOCUMENT

MADISON DISTRICT COURT

CIVIL ACTION FILE NO. 78-C-295

JOHN SMITH Plaintiff vs. JOE JONES, Defendant,	))))))))))	<u>ANSWER AND COUNTERCLAIM</u>

<u>ANSWER</u>

Comes the defendant, Joe Jones, by counsel, and for his answer to the complaint filed herein by plaintiff, alleges and states as follows:

<u>FIRST DEFENSE</u>

The plaintiff's complaint fails to state a claim for which relief may be granted.

<u>SECOND DEFENSE</u>

1) The defendant admits so much of Paragraph 3 of plaintiff's complaint as concerns defendant's employment.

2) Defendant denies each and every other claim and affirmative allegation in plaintiff's complaint.

<u>COUNTERCLAIM</u>

Comes the defendant, Joe Jones, by counsel, and for his counterclaim against the plaintiff, John Smith, states and alleges as follows:

SAMPLE DOCUMENT

1) Defendant, Joe Jones, owns and resides in a certain dwelling located in the City of Waco, Kentucky, at 125 Holly Hill.

2) Plaintiff, John Smith, resides in a house on a tract of land which adjoins the defendant's.

3) Plaintiff, John Smith, owns and controls a certain canine animal.

4) Plaintiff, John Smith, has heretofore willfully permitted said canine animal to run at large and to move onto and about the property owned by plaintiff at will.

5) Said canine animal has on numerous occasions come onto the property owned or controlled by the defendant, and has incessantly and habitually destroyed defendant's laundry hanging on the line, destroyed and eaten Halloween decorations on the porch, destroyed and eaten numerous potted plants, has habitually defecated on or about the premised owned by the defendant, and has habitually overturned defendant's covered garbage receptacle and strewn same around and about defendant's property.

6) Defendant says that the above-mentioned acts occurred because of plaintiff's failure to keep and harbor and control his canine animal as aforesaid, and that because of the plaintiff's failure, the canine animal has been and is now a public nuisance pursuant to 4.32 of the Waco City Code.

7) Because of plaintiff's failure to control his canine animal as aforesaid and because of his willful permission of said animal to do the acts as aforesaid, defendant has incurred actual damages to his property and expenses for repairing and

remedying the damages inflicted by said canine animal in the amount of $1,500.00.

WHEREFORE, the defendant, Joe Jones, demands that plaintiff's complaint herein be dismissed and held naught, that the defendant recover of the plaintiff the sum of $1,500.00 for damages sustained herein, for his costs herein expended, and for all other relief to which defendant may be entitled.

HARRISON & LOGAN
106 Maple Avenue
Waco, Kentucky 40446

CERTIFICATE OF SERVICE

The undersigned attorney for defendant, Joe Jones, hereby certifies that he served the foregoing Answer and Counterclaim on the plaintiff, John Smith, by mailing a true copy thereof to said plaintiff at his last known address of 123 Holly Hill, Waco, Kentucky 40446, on this 14th day of November, 1978.

Larry J. Harrison, Attorney for
Defendant, Joe Jones

Answer and Counterclaim means that he's answering and then suing the plaintiff back.

The "First Defense" is nonsense (quite often indulged in by attorneys)—falls in the ugly neighbor category. For an ugly neighbor lawsuit "First Defense" would be correct.

Paragraph 6 is where the defendant's attorney begins to over-reach himself.

There is no section 4.32 in the City Code.

The section he is refering to is 4.29—"it shall be unlawful for any dog owner to allow his dog to run at large through the city."

The problem this attorney has here is that in this particular city so does everyone else's dog. The law simply is not enforced.

4.29 in a city code simply means Chapter 4, Section 29. If you get hit with something like this just ask the city clerk to show the regulations to you. She has to. It's illegal in this country to have "secret law".

Which leads us to paragraph 7—where this attorney makes a fool of his client. This happens more often than the lawyers want to admit.

The certificate of service merely attests to the fact that the plaintiff was served a copy of the answer and counterclaim. Marshals delivering every scrap of litigation would be ridiculous.

Here's what happened next:

SAMPLE DOCUMENT

MADISON DISTRICT COURT

John Smith, Plaintiff	*	
v	*	Civil Action No. 78-C-295 TRAVERSE TO THE RETURN
Joe Jones, Defendant	*	
	*	

Comes the plaintiff, John Smith, and responds to the defendant's answer and counterclaim seriatim:

1. Disputed issues of fact are to be resolved by a jury

2. Plaintiff denies his White German Shepherd ever destroyed any of defendant's laundry. Defendant's wife quite often hangs up her laundry on an outside line without benefit of clothespins and the wind blows it off. Said laundry is then often left on the ground for days. It is plaintiff's opinion that defendant should have spent some of the alleged $1500 damage money on a drier for his wife.

3. Plaintiff will admit his animal chewed up one (1) Halloween pumpkin belonging to the defendant and is more than willing to pay the fair market value of said pumpkin if the defendant merely informs the plaintiff the replacement cost of said pumpkin.

4. Plaintiff denies his animal destroyed or ate "numerous potted plants" belonging to the defendant for two reasons:

A. The defendant owns only three (3) rather scraggly potted plants visible to the plaintiff.

B. Said potted plants amounted to two (2) until this action was filed. The third plant was placed on the defendant's front porch only after this action was served upon the plaintiff. Said third plant appears

SAMPLE DOCUMENT

to be an indoor plant incapable of surviving a Kentucky winter.

5. Plaintiff denies his animal either habitually overturns defendant's garbage or defecates in his yard and further denies his animal is a public nuisance: even if such allegations were true the defendant had no legal right to abuse said animal.

6. Defendant asserts plaintiff's animal has caused him $1,500.00 actual damages to his property and expenses for repairing and remedying said damages. Plaintiff is somewhat sceptical therefore, under the rules of discovery, plaintiff requests of the defendant the following:

A. An itemized list of all damages done by said animal both as to property damaged and value of same.

B. An itemized list of all repairs made and cost of same that said animal is responsible for.

C. Photostats of all receipts for such repairs.

7. If defendant objects to neighborhood animals traversing his property he has one of two (legal) recourses:

A. Erection of a fence. The previous owner did not do so since the property line of his land was too narrow to drive a truck or other construction equipment into the back yard.

B. Filing a complaint with the proper authorities. However, since all of the Holly St./Holly Hill area is populated by dogs roaming at will it is incumbent upon the defendant to file a complaint against all their owners and not simply discriminate against the plaintiff.

Wherefore, the plaintiff requests trial by jury.

Respectfully Submitted,

John Smith
123 Holly Hill
Waco, Kentucky 40446

SAMPLE DOCUMENT

CERTIFICATE OF SERVICE

This is to certify that I have on this 22nd day of November, 1978, mailed a true and exact copy of the foregoing to counsel for the defense, Larry J. Harrison, 106 Maple Avenue, Waco, Kentucky 40446.

John Smith

That is, the plaintiff said "nonsense" and "prove it". The rules of discovery refer to civil rules, or the rules by which the game is to be played on paper as opposed to the statutes involving jurisdiction or describing what or what does not constitute the rules of acceptable social behavior. It's very similar to chess.

"Discovery" simply means that cross-examination can take place before the case ever goes to trial. If on paper, such discovery is known as interrogatories. If oral, as a deposition.

Now look what defendant's attorney did:

SAMPLE DOCUMENT

MADISON DISTRICT COURT

CIVIL ACTION FILE NO. 78-C-295

JOHN SMITH,	)	
	)	
Plaintiff,	)	
	)	
vs.	)	MOTION TO STRIKE
	)	
JOE JONES,	)	
	)	
Defendant,	)	

Comes the defendant, Joe Jones, by counsel, and moves the Court as follows:

1. For an order striking the pleading filed by the plaintiff herein, entitled "Traverse to the Return", pursuant to C.R. 12.06, because same does not comply with C.R. 7.01 concerning permissible pleadings.

2. For an order striking the following portions of plaintiff's pleading characterized "Traverse to the Return", pursuant to C.R. 12.06, because same is immaterial to the within action.

   a) Second and third sentences of paragraph 2;

   b) Paragraph 4, parts A and B;

   c) Entire portion of paragraph 7.

3. For an order striking so much of paragraph 6 of plaintiff's pleading characterized "Traverse to the Return", pursuant to C.R. 12.06, as purports to request certain items under the Rules of Discovery, on the ground that said request for discovery is not properly presented under the Civil Rules.

HARRISON & LOGAN
106 Maple Avenue
Waco, Kentucky 40446

By: [signature]
Attorneys for Defendant

SAMPLE DOCUMENT

NOTICE OF MOTION

To: Mr. John Smith
123 Holly Hill
Waco, Kentucky 40446

Please take notice that the foregoing Motion to Strike will be brought on for hearing before the District Judge of the Madison District Court, at the Madison County Courthouse, at Richmond, Kentucky, on Thursday, December 21, 1978, at the hour of 1:30 p.m., or as soon thereafter as may be reached by the proceedings of the Court.

Larry J. Harrison, Attorney for
Defendant, Joe Jones

CERTIFICATE OF SERVICE

The undersigned attorney for defendant, Joe Jones, hereby certifies that he served on the foregoing Motion to Strike and Notice thereof upon the plaintiff, John Smith, by mailing a true copy thereof to said plaintiff at his last-known address of 123 Holly Hill, Waco, Kentucky, 40446, on this 27th day of November, 1978.

Larry J. Harrison, Attorney for
Defendant, Joe Jones

"C.R." simply means "civil rules" and in this "motion to strike" (meaning cover it up, get rid of it, etc.) the civil rules had nothing to do with anything concerning the case. Attorneys NEVER admit they make mistakes—they just hide behind numbers and words. Most of which, like smoke, can obscure the scene temporarily but have no substance.

This attorney compounded his mistake by asking for a "status hearing". Since he realized he was in trouble on paper he decided to throw up a verbal smokescreen by dragging the plaintiff into court and intimidating him with his legal wizardry.

The plaintiff countered by requesting a court order forcing the defendant to "fess up" (See page 26).

SAMPLE DOCUMENT

MADISON DISTRICT COURT

John Smith,		
Plaintiff	*	
		Civil Action No. 78-C-295
v	*	MOTION FOR ORDER COMPELLING DISCOVERY
Joe Jones,	*	
Defendant		
	*	

Comes the plaintiff, John Smith, and requests the Court enter an order requiring the defendant to produce the documents and information requested by the plaintiff under the rules of discovery for any and several of the following reasons:

1. Defendant's counsel has refused/evaded such request.

2. Defendant and/or his counsel have apparently filed a sham counterclaim.

3. If said counter-claim is not a sham then the material requested under discovery is absolutely essential to the plaintiff: without it the plaintiff cannot defend himself.

4. Said material is absolutely essential to the plaintiff to demonstrate the motive defendant had in firing upon his White German Shepherd. If no such material exists then an admission of the lack of it goes to impeach defendant's credibility.

Respectfully Submitted,

____
John Smith

This is to certify that I have on this ____ day of December, 1978, mailed a true and exact copy of the foregoing to counsel for the defense, Larry J. Harrison, 106 Maple Avenue, Waco, Kentucky 40446.

John Smith

It blew up in the attorney's face. At the hearing—with judge, stenographer, attorney and plaintiff present—the attorney kept repeating, "I don't know how to cope with this", over and over.

The judge finally ordered him to answer the questions filed for under discovery and dismissed his motion to strike.

The attorney then decided to go for oral discovery from the plaintiff—probably another attempt at legal intimidation — and filed the Notice To Take Deposition shown on the following two pages:

SAMPLE DOCUMENT

MADISON DISTRICT COURT

CIVIL ACTION FILE NO. 78-C-295

JOHN SMITH, PLAINTIFF,

vs. NOTICE TO TAKE DEPOSITION

JOE JONES, DEFENDANT,

*** *** *** *** ***

To: Mr. John Smith
123 Holly Hill
Waco, Kentucky 40446
Plaintiff

Please take notice that the defendant, Joe Jones, will by counsel undersigned, proceed to take the deposition of the plaintiff, John Smith, for the purpose of discovery and for all other purposes consistent with the Rules of Civil Procedure, on Monday, January 29, 1979, at the hour of 4:00 p.m., at the office of Harrison & Logan, 106 Maple Avenue, Waco, Kentucky.

Said deposition shall be taken by an officer authorized to administer oaths.

HARRISON & LOGAN
106 Maple Avenue
Waco, Kentucky 40446

By: Larry J. Harrison
Larry J. Harrison, Attorney for Defendant, Joe Jones

SAMPLE DOCUMENT

CERTIFICATE OF SERVICE

The undersigned attorney hereby certifies that he served the foregoing Notice to Take Deposition on the plaintiff herein by mailing a true copy thereof to said defendant as follows: Mr. John Smith, 123 Holly Hill, Waco, Kentucky, 40446, on this _____ day of January, 1979.

Larry J. Harrison, Attorney for Defendant, Joe Jones

He, the attorney, also decided to answer the interrogatories. Notice how the damages have shrunk.:

SAMPLE DOCUMENT

MADISON DISTRICT COURT

CIVIL ACTION FILE NO. 78-C-295

JOHN SMITH, PLAINTIFF

vs. RESPONSE TO INTERROGATORIES

JOE JONES, DEFENDANT,

*** *** *** *** ***

Comes the defendant, Joe Jones, by counsel, and pursuant to the order of this Court on December 21, 1978, responds to the request for discovery in plaintiff's pleading, which for these purposes, are treated as interrorgatories, as follows:

1. Damages done by animal:

(a) Towel ripped off clothesline and destroyed, $5.00;

(b) On at least ten occasions, has pulled laundry off clothesline, causing the necessity of re-washing same, damaging defendant in the amount of $50.00;

(c) The dog destroyed and ate two pumpkins which were used as Halloween decorations and could be replaced in their state prior to treatment for Halloween purposes at a price of $6.00;

(d) The dog has destroyed one potted palm plant valued at $20.00;

(e) The dog has turned over defendant's covered garbage receptacle and has strewn garbage around and about defendant's property on at least eight occasions. In cleaning up the mess caused by the dog, the defendant has expended his time and energy and that of the members of his family in the reasonable value of $40.00.

(f) The dog has habitually defecated on or about the defendant's property, and in cleaning up same, defendant has expended his time and energy and that of the members of his family in the reasonable value of $50.00.

2. (a) Because of the willful and malicious manner of the plaintiff and of his failure to control his canine animal, defendant has suffered pain and mental anguish, and as reasonable damages therefore, asks for the sum of $500.00; and further requests punitive and exemplary damages in the sum of $500.00.

(b) See a above.

(c) Because of the nature of the damages herein, defendant, Joe Jones, does not have in his possession any receipts referred to in Paragraph C.

HARRISON & LOGAN
106 Maple Avenue
Waco, Kentucky 40446
By: ______________________
Attorneys for Defendant

CERTIFICATE OF SERVICE

The undersigned attorney hereby certifies that he served the foregoing Response to Interrogatories on the plaintiff herein by mailing a true copy thereof to plaintiffs last-known address as follows: Mr. John Smith, 123 Holly Hill, Waco, Kentucky, 40446, on this 2nd day of January, 1979.

____
Larry J. Harrison, Attorney
for Defendant, Joe Jones

Notice paragraph 2(a). On the following four pages you'll see how he keeps digging himself a deeper hole:

SAMPLE DOCUMENT

MADISON DISTRICT COURT

John Smith, Plaintiff v Joe Jones, Defendant	* * * * * * *	Civil Action No. 78-C-295 MOTION TO STRIKE and SECOND SET OF INTERROGATORIES

Comes the plaintiff in the above numbered cause, John Smith, and moves this Court to strike the portion of the pleadings submitted by the defendant in his reponse to interrogatories ordered by this Court alleging that defendant has suffered pain and mental anguish, damages therefore and the request for punitive and exemplary damages for the following reasons:

1. Defendant stated in his original answer and counterclaim that he had "incurred actual damages to his property and expenses for repairing and remedying the damages inflicted by said canine animal in the amount of $1,500." Original answer and counterclaim, page 2, paragraph 7. To change the substance of damages incurred from physical property damage to mental, punitive, and exemplary constitutes an unauthorized amendment of the counterclaim.

2. Such amendment is not allowed without leave of the Court, Civil Rule 15.01.

3. No such leave to amend has even been requested; let alone granted. Further, it is an abuse of discretion to permit a defendant to file an amended answer when he has been guilty of bad faith, see e.g., <u>Lawrence</u> v <u>Marks</u> 355 SW(2d) 162 (1961). Defendant's bad faith should be obvious.

SAMPLE DOCUMENT

SECOND SET OF INTERROGATORIES

Plaintiff is still skeptical as to extent and amount of alleged damages caused by his animal and in order to be able to defend himself requests of the defendant the following information:

1. Color of towel ripped off clothesline:

2. Size of said towel:

3. Cost of towel new:

4. Where towel was purchased:

5. Date towel was purchased:

6. Exact date plaintiff's animal allegedly pulled said towel off of defendant's clothesline:

7. Exact dates of ten occasions plaintiff's animal allegedly pulled laundry off defendant's clothesline:

8. Exactly how damages were computed to amount of $50.00 to laundry:

A. Laundromat fees?

B. Hourly wage?

1. If hourly wage, time required to pick up and clean laundry each time:

9. Exact cost of each pumpkin:

10. From where purchased:

11. Where potted plant was purchased from:

12. Exact cost when purchased:

13. Type of potted plant:

14. Date of purchase:

15. Number of garbage cans owned by defendant:

16. Exact dates of each alleged incident defendant cleaned up after plaintiff's animal?

SAMPLE DOCUMENT

17. How much time in hours and/or minutes expended each time:

18. Dates plaintiff's animal allegedly defecated on defendant's lawn:

19. Time required for each clean-up:

20. Method used to determine plaintiff's animal was actually the guilty party?

A. Observation?

B. Feces sample?

C. Other? Please describe in detail if A, B, or C.

Since the defendant is apparently charging the plaintiff an hourly rate for his alleged services, plaintiff requests:

21. Defendant's rate of pay from I.G.A., computed hourly if possible.

22. Defendant's income from all other sources on an hourly or salary basis:

On the morning of Dec. 6, 1978, at approximately 8 a.m. plaintiff's wife observed a Samoyed Husky belonging to Mrs. Glenda Johnson over-turning the trash can of defendant and telephoned defendant to inform him of same. Defendant then informed plaintiff's wife that he had photos of plaintiff's animal in his trash.

23. Admit or deny such photos exist:

24. Admit or deny whether defendant owns, did own, or possessed at his residence on November 2, 1978 any air-operated pellet or BB pistol or rifle:

Plaintiff hopes he will not have to get another Court Order for discovery but suspects he will have to do so.

Respectfully Submitted,

John Smith

SAMPLE DOCUMENT

CERTIFICATE OF SERVICE

This is to certify that I have on this ____ day of January, 1979, mailed a true and exact copy of the foregoing Motion and Second Set of Interrogatories to counsel for the defense, Larry J. Harrison, 106 Maple Avenue, Waco, Kentucky 40446.

____
John Smith

Finding out what this attorney was doing wrong required less than ten minutes of thumbing through the civil rules and using the index to them. The civil rules for almost any state court at the lower level normally number less than a hundred rules of less than five paragraphs each. In federal court, they are called the Federal Rules of Civil Procedure. If you go to the Federal Appeals Court they are called the Federal Rules of Appellate Procedure.

The case quoted in paragraph 3, *Lawrence* v. *Marks* 355 SW(2d) 162 (1961), means merely that a fellow named Lawrence—back in 1961—got into it with a fellow named Marks. Their case was published in the 355th volume of the SouthWestern Reporter, 2nd Series (there is another set of earlier volumes called the 1st series), on page 162..

The next step was the oral deposition. Since "legal intimidation" had been tried and failed the next step was to try and "trap" the plaintiff. Read the deposition itself and see if you can see what the attorney simply wasn't prepared for:

SAMPLE DOCUMENT

MADISON DISTRICT COURT

CIVIL ACTION FILE NO. 78-C-295

JOHN SMITH, PLAINTIFF,

VS. DEPOSITION OF PLAINTIFF, JOHN SMITH

JOE JONES, DEFENDANT,

*** *** *** ***

The deposition of the plaintiff, John Smith, was taken for the purpose of discovery pursuant to Notice attached hereto, before Doris Childress, Notary Public, in and for the State of Kentucky, at Large, at the Law Offices of Harrison & Logan, at 106 Maple Avenue, Waco, Kentucky, on Monday, January 29, 1979, beginning at the hour of 4:00 p.m., Eastern Standard Time.

APPEARANCES:

JOHN SMITH
123 Holly Hill
Waco, Kentucky 40446
Plaintiff On His Own Behalf

Larry J. Harrison
Attorney for Defendant
106 Maple Avenue
Waco, Kentucky 40446

Joe Jones, Defendant
Waco, Kentucky 40446

The witness, JOHN SMITH, after first being duly sworn, was questioned and testified, as follows:

CROSS EXAMINATION BY LARRY J. HARRISON:

SAMPLE DOCUMENT

1 Would you state your name for the record, please.

A John Smith

2 And where do you live, Mr. Smith?

A I live at 123 Holly Hill in Waco.

3 And what do you do for a living?

A I run a small publishing business.

4 And does that run out of your home?

A Yes, it is.

5 And are you married, Mr. Smith?

A Yes, I am.

6 This, the basis of this lawsuit apparently concerns a dog, and I suppose that you own a certain dog now, do you not?

A Yes, that's correct.

7 What kind of dog do you own?

A It's a light german shepherd.

8 And what, how big of an animal is it?

A How big at the incident, or how big is he now?

9 Both.

A At the time of the incident, I guess he, I think he weighed about fifty-four pounds, and now I think he weighs around ninety, but I am not sure.

10 How old of a dog is it?

A Right now, It's ten months.

11 Where did you buy the dog? Where did you obtain the dog?

A From a fella up in Lexington, I can't recall his name off hand. It's on his papers.

SAMPLE DOCUMENT

11 Did you buy the dog or were you given, or was it given to you?

A I bought it.

12 And how much did you pay for it?

A Hundred dollars.

13 Is he registered with the A.K.C.?

A Yes he is.

14 And do you have papers on him?

A Yes, I do.

15 What's his registered name, do you know?

A S Hugh Dillin.

16 You want to spell that for her?

A Just S. Then the next one is H-U-G-H, and the next one is D-I-L-L-I-N.

17 Do you have a Kentucky, current Kentucky license on the animal?

A Yes, I do.

18 And he has been vaccinated I suppose?

A No, he hasn't.

19 Do you own the property on which your house sits, Mr. Smith?

A No, my mother does.

20 O.K. Now do you lease your house from her, or does she live with you, or ....?

A No, I rent from her.

21 O.K. Do you know how large the lot is on which your house is located?

A Probably, approximately half an acre, but I couldn't say for sure.

22 Do you know the dimensions, frontages or how deep the lot is?

A No.

23 How big is your yard?

A I don't know exactly.

24 Do you have a fence around your yard?

A No, I don't.

25 Do you have a dog house for the animal to stay in?

A Yes, I do.

26 Do you let the dog in the house?

A Yes.

27 Do you tie the dog up ever?

A No.

28 Do you have any method of restraining the dog?

A Yes, Newspaper.

29 Does the dog, so far as you know, ever leave your property?

A Occasionally.

30 And, if he does so, there is normally no method to keep him on the property other than the newspaper that you refer to?

A No, because we have him, we've got him pretty well trained. It's like, if he starts across the street, all we have to do is tap on the window, and he knows

SAMPLE DOCUMENT

he's not supposed to cross the street, and he'll come back.

31 But, you don't always observe him, I suppose....

A Oh, no.

32 Since you said that he did go off occasionally?

A No.

33 In connection with the complaint that you filed, here, in specifically, Paragraph seven, wherein you allege that Mr. Jones essentially shot your dog with a pellet pistol, I wish you'd tell me please whether you in fact yourself saw this act?

A No, my wife saw it when the dog got hit.

34 And where was your dog when it got hit, according to your wife?

A It was either in my backyard or his backyard, had to be one of the two.

35 You don't know which?

A No.

36 Did anyone else see it, so far as you know?

A No, not as far as I know.

37 What did your wife tell you that the dog did? What did she tell you she saw?

A Well, as close as I can remember...now do you want me to play he says, she says, or do you want to get a deposition from her?

38 Well, I may have to take her deposition, but I want to know on what you're basing the claim, okay?

SAMPLE DOCUMENT

A Okay. Well, basically what happened was this.
She was standing next to the stove. The backdoor
was open, the kitchen door was open. Now when
our backdoor and our kitchen door is open, you
can see out to both yards, because there is also
a window. You see like directly into his backyard
and you see directly into my backyard. The dog was
back there some place. Now, I am not sure exactly.
It could have been his backyard. I don't know. She
saw the dog jump up and yelp. She thought at the
time that he'd scratched himself on a piece of barb
wire or something like that. So, the dog came back
in. He had a big spot of blood on him, about the size
of a teacup, and we didn't think anything of it. We
thought he'd just cut himself, but she'd know
when he was hurt, because she saw, she saw
him yelp. He came in with that spot of blood.
About eight o'clock that night, she decided to clean
the wound, and when she started pulling it apart, a
pellet fell out, and she immediately put two and two
together because the only place that he could have
been hit with that pellet was from somebody standing on
his backporch firing the weapon. So she went over there
and she asked him, you know, why'd you shoot my dog.
I don't know what else came of it, because he didn't stand
to talk to her, his wife did, and she said, well no,
it couldn't have been him because his pellet pistol was
still packed away. But that's the basis of the complaint.

SAMPLE DOCUMENT

39 She did not, then, so far as you know, see a weapon discharged from Mr. Jones's backporch or anyone else's?

A That, well, no she didn't see the weapon discharged say from his backporch, because when you're standing like in our kitchen, somebody could shoot a howitzer from his backporch, and you couldn't see who it was because it's, it's semi-enclosed, at least there is just no direct line of vision there. She did go talk to several of the neighbors, you know, trying to trace it down before she went to talk to him.

40 Did you take the dog to a veterinarian?

A No.

41 Do you have any photographs of the dog at anywhere near to the time of the incident or specifically, after the time of the incident which show the alleged injury?

A No, but I have witnesses. I have other people that saw the injury.

42 Please tell me who saw the injury?

A Nancy Rawlings saw it, in fact, she mentioned it. She said what's the problem, and I think there are a couple of other people, but I'm not sure. I know for sure that she saw the injury.

43 Where does she live?

A She lives on Holly Street or Hanson Street. She's right across the street from us. Her husband owns the Central Service Station.

SAMPLE DOCUMENT

44 But you did not seek medical treatment for the dog after it was, it received this injury?

A No.

45 Did you buy any medicine or anything?

A No.

46 Has the dog recovered?

A Yes he has.

47 Is there any evidence of the wound?

A We still have the pellet, that's all, and the, and the witnesses, and that's about the extent of it.

48 How about on the dog's body, is there any evidence of this injury?

A I wouldn't know unless I parted the hair back and looked.

49 Does he exhibit any, any physical difficulties as a result of this injury?

A No.

50 Has the dog then, would you say that the dog has, is the same as if he had not received the injury, so far as you know?

A Physically or mentally?

51 Well, physically, since I think that's probably all that's...

A Animals can get treacherous if you abuse them, but I'd say physically he's the same.

52 Well what about now, do you think he's the same?

SAMPLE DOCUMENT

A I know he is scared of him. Every time he gets out in his car, the dog runs for it.

53 When you say "him", do you mean Mr. Jones?

A Right.

54 Any other evidences of alteration of behavior?

A No, not that I know of.

55 Is the dog a lovable dog, would you say?

A Oh, I would say so. It's good with kids.

56 And does it ever have any problems with children or any adults for that matter? Has it ever bitten anyone?

A No.

57 Ever attacked anyone?

A No.

58 So, would you say that it's a gentle dog now?

A That's a difficult question because when somebody gets near the kids, he gets ugly if he doesn't know them, but as far as people he knows, yeah.

59 And would you say that his behavioral patterns are about the same, given the, the maturing process, now as they were before this injury?

A Mm huh (yes), about the same.

60 Did you ever see your dog on Mr. Jones's property?

A Of course. The previous owner wanted us to train him to go on his property, because he was afraid of burglars.

61 Of course, Mr. Jones never asked you to do that, did he?

SAMPLE DOCUMENT

A No, Mr. Jones never said anything to me even after the time he shot my dog.

62 And how many times would you say that you saw the dog on his property?

A Well, going across it, I'd say it'd have to be a bunch of times.

63 Well is a bunch a dozen, or twenty or fifty?

A Oh, I don't know. It could be a dozen times in a given forty-eight hour period.

64 Did you ever have any complaints from anyone about your dog?

A No.

65 No one at all?

A No one at all.

66 I think you, in the document which you entitled "Traverse to the Return, Paragraph three, admitted that your dog did chew up one pumpkin?

A Right.

67 That Mr. Jones owned?

A Yes.

68 Could you tell me how you know this?

A I don't know. I think one of the kids observed it, I'm not sure.

69 One of your children?

A Yes, but I do know that our dog did eat one pumpkin of his.

70 Okay, and where was the pumpkin located as far as you know?

SAMPLE DOCUMENT

A It was on his front porch.

71 Has anyone investigated any of this either on your behalf or, well on your behalf, besides yourself?

A As far as to what?

72 Well, as far as to any of the claims made in this lawsuit. Have you had anyone investigate it for you?

A No.

73 Do you know, Mr. Smith, whether your wife ever went onto Mr. Jones's property and cleaned it up after...?

A Numerous times, in fact, quite a few times, Glenda Johnson's dog would come down there and knock over his trash can, and we thought it was our dog, I suspect our dog did it once or twice, and she'd go out and clean up after him, and December 6th, she saw Glenda Johnson's dog out there in the actual act of knocking over . . . and she called Mr. Jones here and told him that she wouldn't clean it up because it wasn't our dog that did it.

74 Do you know of your own knowledge, or do you have reason to believe that your dog has, in fact, been into his garbage can?

A Oh, of course, and if Glenda Johnson's dog knocks it over, a dog is a natural scavenger, it's going to go after whatever is laying around.

75 Well do you know whether your dog has ever knocked it over?

A I have never seen him. No, I don't.

76 Well, do you know why your wife did go onto his property and clean up some trash?

A We just naturally assumed it was our dog.

77 Do you know, of your own knowledge, whether your wife ever told Mr. Jones's wife that your dog had knocked over the garbage and she was cleaning up because of him?

A Yes, more than likely.

: : MR. HARRISON. That's all.

DEPOSITION CONCLUDED.

SAMPLE DOCUMENT

REPORTER'S CERTIFICATE

I, Doris Childress, the undersigned Notary Public in and for the State of Kentucky at Large, do certify that the facts contained in the caption hereto are true; that at the time and place stated, the witness named in the caption hereto personally appeared before me, and after being by me duly sworn, was examined by counsel for defendant; that said testimony was taken down in shorthand by me and later reduced to typewriting; and the foregoing is a true record of the testimony given by said witness.

No party to said action, nor counsel for said parties requested in writing that this deposition be signed by testifying witness.

My commission expires: November 6, 1982.

IN TESTIMONY WHEREOF, I have hereunto set my hand and seal of office, this 1st day of February, 1979.

Doris Childress
Doris Childress, Notary Public
State-at-Large, Kentucky

Reporter's Fee:

Taking Deposition --	$25.00
Transcribing Original & Certificate, 16 pages at $1.30 ea. -	$20.80
TOTAL ----------	$45.80

He wasn't prepared for honest and forthright answers. Attorneys spend so much time lying to themselves, each other, and their clients that they are generally unable to cope with anyone telling the truth. It's a shattering experience for many of them.

What this attorney was apparently hoping for was that the plaintiff would indulge in some rather gross prevarications about the damage done to his dog.

Sometimes this can become a trifle tricky. The issue here was *not* the damage done to the dog—it was the unlawful behavior of the defendant.

Quite often attorneys get so far afield in trying to muddle the issues that you have to bring them back on track with a "statement of genuine issues". Had it been necessary in this case it simply would have been filed as a motion with questions for the court to consider:

1. Did the defendant's conduct constitute unlawful behavior?

2. Did the defendant's conduct constitute grounds for a civil action?

3. Does this court have jurisdiction?

Etc.

Let him explain the "animal wasn't really hurt" and so on to a jury.

In your case, try not to lie. Makes it easier to remember what you said.

The last thing filed in this case was defendant's answer to interrogatories. No court order was necessary.

SAMPLE DOCUMENT

MADISON DISTRICT COURT

CIVIL ACTION FILE NO. 78-C-295

JOHN SMITH, Plaintiff, vs. JOE JONES, Defendant,	)))))))))))	<u>ANSWERS TO INTERROGATORIES</u>

Comes the defendant, Joe Jones, by counsel, and for answers to the interrogatories filed on January 15, 1979 by the plaintiff, states as follows:

1. Unknown
2. Specific size of the towel is unknown, however, it was a face towel.
3. About $4.00 to $5.00.
4. Unknown .
5. Unknown.
6. Several occasions in October and November, 1978; exact dates unknown.
7. Several occasions in October and November, 1978; exact dates unknown.
8. The sum is comparable to the amount which would be charged for cleaning by commercial laundry or dry-cleaning.
9. $2.59 each.
10. IGA, Waco, Kentucky.

SAMPLE DOCUMENT

11. The plant was purchased from a Mr. Abney, who was driving a truck through Waco for a Florida nursery.

12. $17.50.

13. Some type of palm.

14. August or September, 1978.

15. One.

16. Several occasions during October, November, and December, 1978.

17. Approximately twenty minutes.

18. Several occasions in October, November, and December, 1978.

19. Approximately twenty minutes.

20. Direct observation.

21. Defendant objects to the discovery of the information requested in this interrogatory on the ground the same is not discoverable under CR 26.

22. Defendant objects to the discovery of the information requested in this interrogatory on the ground the same is not discoverable under CR 26.

23. Admit.

24. Admit.

HARRISON & LOGAN
106 Maple Avenue
Waco, Kentucky 40446

By: ______________________
Attorneys for Defendant

SAMPLE DOCUMENT

The undersigned attorney for defendant hereby certifies that he served the foregoing Answers to Interrogatories upon the plaintiff herein by mailing a true copy thereof to said plaintiff, John Smith, 123 Holly Hill, Waco, Kentucky, 40446, on this ____ day of February, 1979.

Attorney for Defendant

While this case—at the moment—is still pending the plaintiff—up to now—has "won" as far as simply getting even goes. His expenses—since he did his own legal work—were less than $50.00. The defendant—paying an attorney at the current rate of $50.00 an hour—had to run his expenses into the hundreds of dollars.

3. Self-Defense

Occasionally, someone may try to land on you with both legal feet. You may be on the receiving end of a lawsuit.

Normally, at least in small cases, what happens is the attorney for the defendant milks the defendant for all the money he thinks he can get in "legal fees" and then tells him, "I've done all I can, I think we had better settle out of court".

Translated, the defendant will wind up shelling out MORE money—only this time to the OTHER attorney. One-third for the other attorney, two-thirds to his client.

It's cheaper to counter-sue. Of course, that involves a lot more work for the defendant's attorney and is normally not indulged in. The attorney in the previous case in Chapter II thought he had a "piece of cake" (i.e., the legal eagle vs. the poor, stupid, dumb uneducated non-lawyer) and apparently—once he realized that he had fallen into a pit he dug for himself—was unable to back up and save face in time.

Let's take a typical example. This case was filed in Small Claims Court. If you think the other side has any political clout at all, avoid it—and anything like it—the way you would leprosy. Any time you submit to trial by judge—which is what you're doing in small claims court—the case can be adjudicated merely by the whim or caprice of the judge. This is also true occasionally of juries but at least your chances are twelve times better.

The case following was filed against me on 12-28-78 in Madison County and I was served with it via certified mail.

The documents appearing on the following pages look official and imposing, don't they?

SAMPLE DOCUMENT

AOC-78-111 Commonwealth of Kentucky Court of Justice	SMALL CLAIMS SUMMONS	Case No. 78-S-254 County Madison Court District

B & J Quick Print — **Plaintiff**
211 Geri Lane
Richmond, Kentucky 40475

VS.

Madison Company — **Defendant**
101 Cherry Street
Berea, Kentucky 40403

The Commonwealth of Kentucky

To The Above-Named Defendant(s):

You are hereby notified that a legal action has been filed against you in this court demanding relief as shown on the document delivered to you with this summons.

You are summoned to appear before this court on February 15, 19 79 at 9:30A M. at the following location Madison District Court; Madison County Courthouse.

Failure to appear on the date indicated may result in a judgment by default for the relief demanded in the attached complaint.

The name(s) and address(es) of the party or parties demanding such relief against you or his (their) attorney(s) are shown on the document delivered to you with this summons.

Date December 29, 1978 Edric W. Newman, by:
Clerk
Janice L. Dremer, D.C.

PROOF OF SERVICE

This summons was served by delivering a true copy and the complaint (or other initiating document) to: ____________________

____

This ________ day of ____________________, 19____.

Served by: ____________________

SAMPLE DOCUMENT

AOC-77-101

Commonwealth of Kentucky
Court of Justice

SMALL CLAIMS COMPLAINT

Case No. 78-S-254
Rec # 304957
Rec'd 13.00

In the Small Claims Division, District Court, of Madison County

Plaintiff S & J. Quick Print
Address 211 Geri Ln.
Richmond, Ky 40475

Attorney (If Any) Open Court
Date 12-28-78
Time 3:30pm. Filed

Defendant Madison Company
Address 101 Cherry St
Berea, Ky 40403

Attorney (If Any) Att: Edric W. Newman, C.M.C.C.
By: D.C.

NOTICE TO EACH DEFENDANT — READ CAREFULLY

You are being sued in the Small Claims Division of District Court by the Plaintiff(s) shown above. The judge has not made any decision in this case. You are to appear in the court on the date shown on the attached summons to tell your side of the dispute.

However, if you fail to appear in court on the date shown on the attached summons a court judgment can be taken against you for the money or property demanded in the following complaint. This could lead to garnishment of your pay check and/or sale of your home or other belongings (unless protected by law) to satisfy that judgment.

If you have questions or need assistance, consult the Small Claims Information pamphlet or call an attorney.

Complaint

1. Plaintiff claims that the defendant owes for printing

2. Plaintiff claims the following sum from the defendant for damages brought by the above complaint; $ 244.35.

3. Plaintiff also claims court cost. ✓

Edric W. Newman
Clerk
Address Courthouse
Richmond, Ky.
623-6732
Phone number

Jim Blake
Plaintiff's Signature or Attorney

12-28-78
Date of Filing

-3-

(See Reverse)

SAMPLE DOCUMENT

Small Claims Affidavit

KRS 24A.250

(1) "No party shall file more than twenty-five claims in any one calendar year in the Small Claims Division of any district court in the Commonwealth. Any business engaged in trade or commerce shall be entitled to the maximum number of claims allowed under this section of this Act for each established location in the district that has been engaged in trade or commerce for at least six months."

I swear (or affirm) that I have not brought more than the maximum number of claims allowed under KRS 24A.250(7).

Jim Blake

(Name and Date)

Subscribed and sworn to and before me by

Jim Blake this 28 day of December, 19 78.

Edric W. Newman

(Signature)

Clerk

Title

Janice L. Dunn

By D.C.

WARNING

KRS 24A.320

"All claims in the Small Claims Division shall be tried without jury. Upon filing a claim, the plaintiff shall be deemed to have waived his right to a jury trial in the Division."

In this case, the court clerk stuck in a little green booklet explaining how the small claims court worked.

As you can probably guess by the answer and counter-claim I wasn't much interested in playing the games he thought we were going to play:

SAMPLE DOCUMENT

MADISON DISTRICT COURT

B & J Quick Print, Plaintiff	*	
	*	
v	*	Case No. 78-S-254
Madison Company, Defendant	*	

ANSWER AND COUNTERCLAIM

Comes the defendant, through its owner Michael H. Brown, and for its defense deposes and states as follows:

1. The Small Claims Court does not have jurisdiction of this cause in the instant case since the defendant demands trial by jury. $12.50 fee for such trial is enclosed.

2. The plaintiff, evidently represented by its owner Jim Blake, has filed a perjurious affidavit.

A. Plaintiff's original bill was for $262.50.

B. Defendant has canceled checks in his possession made to plaintiff for said bill in excess of $100.00.

C. Plaintiff has repeatedly tried to "pad" said bill, as he has evidently done in Small Claims Court.

FACTS

3. Lani Brown, co-owner of Madison Company, originally ordered one thousand (1,000) shipping labels from the plaintiff for an agreed-upon price of $26.25.

4. Plaintiff made a "mistake" and printed 10,000 labels.

5. Defendant, at the time believing said "mistake" to be an honest one, agreed to take the 9,000 excess labels.

6. In conversations with other businessmen defendant discovered that such "mistakes" are chronic with the plaintiff.

7. Defendant then ceased payment on said bill.

8. Plaintiff is more than welcome to take back the 9,000 excess labels, many of which are so poorly printed as to be unusable.

LEGAL CLAIMS

9. The actions of the plaintiff constitute the torts of:

A. Deceit. There was an intentional misrepresentation with intent to mislead by the use of false statements. The element of scienter is self-evident in the instant case.

B. Filing an affidavit the plaintiff knows to be false constitutes the tort known as abuse of process.

10. Such unethical and patently unlawful conduct on the part of the plaintiff allows the defendant to file a counterclaim for damages.

RELIEF REQUESTED

1. Compensatory damages in the amount of $300.00.
2. Punitive damages in the amount of $1200.00.
3. Trial by jury on all issues triable by jury.

Respectfully Submitted,

Michael H. Brown
Owner
Madison Company
101 Cherry Road
Berea, Kentucky
40403

SAMPLE DOCUMENT

CERTIFICATE OF SERVICE

This is to certify that I have on this ____ day of January, 1979, placed a true and exact copy of the foregoing pleading in the U.S. Mails addressed to plaintiff, B & J Quick Print, 211 Geri Lane, Richmond, Kentucky 40475.

Michael H. Brown

FIRST SET OF INTERROGATORIES

1. Give names, addresses, and amounts owed of all other defendants sued by B & J Quick Print in Small Claims Court in 1978 and 1979 and all such information regarding defendants to be sued in 1979 where service of process has not been effected.

2. Give names and addresses of all customers of B & J Quick Print from Jan. 1, 1978 to date.

Such information is necessary to defendant in order to subpoena witnesses and take depositions proving the dishonesty of the plaintiff.

The demand for jury trial is an absolute right—in controversies involving amounts over $20.00—guaranteed by the Seventh Amendement, U.S. Constitution. Practically all state courts will honor it. Almost no federal courts will unless you're IBM or somebody.

The interrogatories can sometimes solve a double purpose. In this case if I could have gotten the names and addresses of all his customers, I could have sold them to another printing business. However, I never filed a motion to compel the plaintiff to answer the interrogatories since in this case all I wanted to do was get the plaintiff off my back.

It's been two years since he sued me in Small Claims Court and I haven't heard a peep out of him. Must have worked.

Finally, on the following page you'll see what court clerks do for you. I made a filing mistake and she's helping me to clean it up.

SAMPLE DOCUMENT

COMMONWEALTH OF KENTUCKY
EDRIC W. NEWMAN, CLERK
MADISON CIRCUIT COURT
RICHMOND, KENTUCKY 40475

MADISON COUNTY COURTHOUSE

TELEPHONE NUMBERS
(606) 623-2760
(606) 623-3174

Mr. Brown -

There is $15.00 more due on this case. The reason for this is because your counterclaim ask for $1500. This moves the case from Small Claims division to Civil division.

I only filed your answer - I will file your counterclaim when I receive the money.

Thank you -

4. Reading The Law

Once you have mastered the English language—something most of us master in grade school—the only thing remaining necessary to "law" somebody (as they say here in Kentucky) is a knowledge of the indexing system. All American law books are indexed, cross-indexed, and use references of one sort or another so extensively that it is almost impossible not to find what you are looking for.

However, occasionally there are even easier ways to do things than rummage through the law books.

Let's say you want to form a corporation. The first and most obvious step is to hire a lawyer, let him shuffle a few papers for you, and write him a check for upwards of $500.00.

Which means you just paid upwards of $450.00 too much.

The least expensive and easiest way to incorporate is to walk into the County Clerk's office—that's the one in the vault where all the mortgages, deeds, and so forth are kept—and ask to see the book containing corporations recently formed. It is normally titled "Articles" (for Articles of Incorporation). What they will have on file is the original application with a notarized signature of the person who filed the papers and a State seal, often consisting of less than three pages. Normally there will be a copy machine close by. Pick out a corporation that you can use as a blueprint for your own, have it copied—usually about $.50 a page—and stick in your own corporate name. A letter to the State Capitol, usually addressed to the Secretary of State, will let you know what the filing fees are. Normally such fees are around $20.00. In Kentucky and most other states, the Secretary of State publishes a corporation book that makes the job even easier since they are usually well-indexed, contain all the applicable laws in one volume, and even tell you the books which have samples of the forms you may need or the laws of other states. Counting the filing fee, copy expense, postage, parking near the county courthouse, and two or three hours of your time figured at $10.00 an hour you should be able to wrap the whole affair up for less than $50.00.

Let's say you want to familiarize yourself with the federal laws concerning treason. What you are doing here is going through the procedure step-by-step. When you finish this chapter you should be able to use this same procedure for almost any legal question you may have.

The emphasis may appear to be on the federal system.

It isn't. Not in this chapter.

I am simply using the federal system to teach you the "ropes" because all of the fifty states use almost exactly the same indexing systems.

Here's what you do. Let's say you want to look up "treason"—what it is defined as legally, what the government definition of it is, how the courts have treated it, and so forth.

Step No. 1: Where to look.

Every county courthouse in the United States contains a law library. Quite often the less populated counties contain merely a haphazard collection of out-dated and dis-organized law books and are not worth visiting. The larger cities are often quite sophisticated and professional. Lexington, Kentucky, for example has a law library on the fourth floor of the county courthouse that is quite extensive. It contains, in additional to the Kentucky Laws and Reporters, all the Federal Law and form books most anyone would ever need to use. If you want to know where a particular set of books are covering a particular subject all you have to do is ask the librarian.

Quite often you can find the exact same sets of books in a university library; always if it is a law school. A school that has a law library and no law school (such as Eastern

Kentucky University, Richmond, Kentucky) is the easiest to work in—nobody ever uses it and gets underfoot.

The worst places are ones like Dayton, Ohio. There the county law library—in a building (the county courthouse) paid for by the taxpayers only admitted members of the bar (lawyers) are allowed to use the law library. This is illegal and unconstitutional but lawyers are not exactly the most law-abiding class of people around. It's hard to make them behave.

If you go to the county law library somewhere other than Dayton you can simply look at the signs on the walls telling you where everything is. The only other method I know of is to walk around until you find a room full of books that is also full of hatchet-faced young men cruising around in sharkskin suits looking like it is feeding time at the aquarium. Those are lawyers in a law library.

Don't feel bad about walking in without a suit and tie. You'll get some strange looks but not for the reason you expect. Most of them will just figure you're a HEAVY criminal attorney working on a narcotics case; making so much money you can flaunt convention. A killer whale.

Step No. 2: Where to start.

In almost every law library there is a collection of a collection of books published by West Publishing Company, 50 West Kellogg Blvd., St. Paul, Minn. Walk around the law library until you see a set of books burgundy or maroon in color. Facing you on the binding will be the following letters in this form:

U
S
C
A

Underneath "USCA", which stands for "United States Code Annotated" will be a number, in numbers the same size as the letters in USCA, anything from 1 up to and including 50, or the word "INDEX". It will look something like this:

U
S
C
A
—
18

The "18" is the number of the United States Code outlining crimes and criminal procedure. "28" outlines the judiciary and judical procedure, "47" telegraphs, telephones, and radiotelegraphs, and so forth. For example, 18 U.S.C. 241 means Title 18, crimes and criminal procedure, Section 241, conspiracy. The "A" is not used on legal documents since it simply refers to "annotated", or cases West Publishing printed to explain the various court interpretations of that particular part of the Code. Lawyers Co-operative, another law book publishing firm, uses "USCS" which means "United States Code Service".

Step No. 3: Using the USCA Index.

Pick up the INDEX volume (all INDEX volumes will be found at the end of the U.S. Code) labeled S to T. There are two sets of indexes. One for the U.S. Code, one for the Constitution.

Use it just the way you would any other index.

Turn to "T" for treason.

What you will see looks like this:

TREASON
Constitution of United States, provisions of concerning. See Index to Constitution Volume
Counsel and witnesses, 18 § 3005
Customs officers aiding importation of treasonous literature, penalty, 18 § 552
Defined, 18 § 2381

Misprision of treason, 18 § 2382
Extradition,
State, territory or possession into extraterritorial jurisdiction of United States, 18 § 3183
State or territory to state, district or territory, 18 § 3182
Federal employees, conviction, forteiture of annuities and retired pay, 5 § 8312
Federal old age, survivors or disability insurance benefits, 42 § 402
Importation of book advocating prohibited, 19 § 1305

The first two numbers refer to a title of the U.S. Code. The § is an abbreviation for "section". The numbers after § are specific sections of that title. For example, Title 18 is the U.S. Criminal Code, Title 5 is Government Organization and Employees, Title 42 is the Public Health and Welfare, and Title 19 is Customs Duties. All of these titles are listed at the front of each volume.

Step No. 4: Reading the Cases.

Put the INDEX volume back and go to the volumes labeled "Title 18". Each volume has numbers indicating one section to another section.

"Treason defined" leads us to Title 18, Section 2381.

2381. Treason

Whoever, owing allegiance to the United States, levies war against them or adheres to their enemies, giving them aid and comfort within the United States or elsewhere, is guilty of treason and shall suffer death, or shall be imprisoned not less than five years and fined not less than $10,000; and shall be incapable of holding any office under the United States.

Other similar crimes will usually be lumped together in a series:

Sec.
2381. Treason
2382. Misprision of treason.
2383. Rebellion or insurrection.
2384. Seditious conspiracy.
2385. Advocating overthrow of Government.
2386. Registration of certain organizations.
2387. Activities affecting armed forces generally.
2388. Activities affecting armed forces during war.
2389. Recruiting for service against United States.
2390. Enlistment to serve against United States.
2391. Temporary extension of section 2388.

After this there will be a legislative history of the law and an extensive index. The index will then be broken down into subdivisions. They (all indexes) look something like this:

Constitutionality 1
Construction of constitutional provision 2
Geographical application 4
Naturalization 5
Power of Congress 3
Territorial application 4

The numbers to the right in the index are found on the left in the cases that match them. For example, "Constitutionality 1" leads you to:

1. Constitutionality

This section was not unconstitutional as a denial of due process when applied to American citizen of Japanese ancestry who allegedly broadcasted on radio during war from Japan to members of the American armed forces in Pacific ocean area with intent to destroy their confidence and undermine their morale, because this section was not applicable to a former American citizen who had become a naturalized citizen of Japan. Iva Ikuko Toguri D'Aquino v. U.S., C.A.Cal. 1951, 192, F.2d 338, rehearing denied

203 F.2d 390, certiorari denied 72 S. Ct. 772, 343 U.S. 935, 96 L.Ed. 1343, rehearing denied 72 S. Ct. 1053, 343 U.S. 958, 96 L.Ed. 1358, rehearing denied 73 S.Ct. 786, 345 U.S. 931, 97 L.Ed. 1361.

Some of you younger readers may remember seeing this case on "60 Minutes". Some of you older ones may have heard her in the Pacific. This was "Tokyo Rose".

Before you accept anything you read in the main volume as gospel, check the pocket part. That's a part of the volume updated every year and slipped into a "pocket" in the back. In this case there doesn't seem to have been much treason going on lately. The closest we can come is a little rebellion or insurrection:

2383. Rebellion or insurrection

Supplementary Index to Notes

Elements of Offense 6
Search and seizure 7

6. Elements of offense
Attempt of domestic organizations to attack and subvert existing structure of government is not a crime unless the activity is carried on through unlawful means, such as invasion of rights of others by use of force or violence. U.S. v. Sinclair, D.C. Mich. 1971, 321 F.Supp. 1074.

Step No. 5: What is 321 F.Supp. 1074?

In any "case cite", as lawyers refer to them, the first set of numbers refers to the volume number, the words or abbreviations of words refer to the series of volumes that case is found in, and the last set of numbers merely refers to the page number the case begins on. That is, 321 F.Supp. 1074 is volume 321 of the Federal Supplements with *U.S.* v *Sinclair* being the case beginning on page 1074.

Further case breakdowns are as follows:

343 U.S. 935 is the 343rd volume of the United States Reports, page 935. "U.S." used like this is always a Supreme Court of the United States case.

72 S. Ct. 772 is the same case in volume 72 of the Supreme Court reporter, page 772.

96 L.Ed. 1358 is the same case as the foregoing two in volume 96 of the Lawyer's Edition, page 1358.

All of these are U.S. Supreme Court decisions (or citations) and as such are binding on both federal (when they feel like it) and state courts. The Tokyo Rose decision isn't binding or anything since "certiorari denied" simply means the Supreme Court declined to hear the case. You have an absolute right of appeal to every higher court in the nation except that one.

To get to the Supreme Court, a case either has to have been appealed from a State Supreme Court or from a Federal Court of Appeals. In the above case the appeal was from a Federal Court of Appeals since 203 F 2d 390 means the case was published in volume 203 of the Federal Reporter, Second Series, page 390. Not all cases are published. Generally speaking, the cases that make it into the Federal Reporters and Federal Supplements are meant to serve as "guide" to the rest of the legal profession, interpreting existing law and showing how it is to be applied.

Federal Reporters are published for Federal Courts of Appeals, Federal Supplements for District Court decisions. A Federal Court of Appeals can overturn a District Court decision and the Supreme Court can overturn the Court of Appeals decision.

State cases and statutes are similar in arrangement to the Federal system. Most States have either "Annotated Codes" such as California does, or "Revised Statutes", like Kentucky. The reason they are usually called "Revised" in many States is that such laws were set down in the 19th century and merely revised from time to time. Kentucky in 1976, for example, revised its criminal statutes and threw out everything having to do with lewd cohabitation.

A California case cite would look like this:
People v. Mahoney, 1975, 122 Cal. Rptr. 174, 47 C.A. 3d 699. Translated, the case was decided in 1975 and published in volume 122 of the California Reporter, page 174, and apparently a lower court case since it was appealed and that decision was published in volume 47 of the Court of Appeals, Third Series, page 699. Higher-ranking courts are always given last or to the right of courts of inferior jurisdiction.

Typical legal volume abbreviations are as follows:

A2d Atlantic Reporter, Second Series. This set of cases would cover several individual states on the Eastern Seaboard.

ALR 2d American Law Reports, Second Series. This set of books covers various fields in extreme depth, including actual trial testimony. ALR 3d is a good example: one question discussed is whether hospital records in certain circumstances may be used as evidence in a criminal trial.

CA 3d California Appellate Reports, Third Series. See example previously given.

D.C.D.C. District of Columbia District Court (Federal).

FRD Federal Rules Decisions, or how the Federal Courts apply the Federal Rules of Civil Procedure and other administrative matters.

U2d Utah Reports, Second Series.

Utah is good for research on polygamy cases since the federal government hasn't bothered itself about it since 1946, the U.S. Supreme Court since 1886.

Step No. 6: The West Key System

Pull volume 321 of the Federal Supplements from the bookshelf. Federal Supplements and Federal Reporters are easy to recognize: they are rather thick, large volumes, gold in color, with a red band about four inches wide on the "spine" or back of the book. Inside the red band is the volume number and designation, looking like this:

321
F Supp

Turn to page 1074 in volume 321 of the Federal Supplements. What you now have is an in-depth summary of that particular case and how the issues of law were interpreted. If you want to dig into the case even further you can buy every motion filed, every word of testimony, and every countermotion from the court clerk or court stenographer. For $.50 a page. But make sure you write or call the court where the case was adjudicated. The Lexington, Kentucky Court cannot retrieve records for you from the District of Columbia District Court.

There will be a series of short paragraphs preceeded by heavy black printed numbers, a word, a drawing of a key, and a one to three digit number to the right of the key. It will look something like this:

1. Criminal Law 🔑 627.7(1)
   Government must disclose and make available to a defendant who has proper standing any conversations in which he participated or which occurred on his premises and were overheard by government during course of any illegal electronic surveillance. U.S.C.A. Court Amend. 4.

What the key refers to is Modern Federal Practice Digest, section 627.7 also published by West.

🔑 627. Service of copy of Indictment information, or or minutes of evidence.
 Library references
  C.J.S. Criminal Law 941 et. seq.
🔑 627(1). In general.

D.C.N.H. 1953. The showing of a copy of the indictment to defendant's counsel was a substantial and effective compliance with rule requiring that defendant be given a copy of indictment or information before he is called upon to plead. Fed. Rules Crim.Proc. rule 10, 18, U.S.C.A.
U.S. v Shepherd, 108 F.Supp. 721.

627(2). Necessity to serve.

And so on. For later cases go to 627 in the pocket part. As in USCA, the pocket part for this series of volumes is updated once a year.

For State cases, as opposed to Federal, C.J.S. and ALR 3d are quite good. ALR 3d has already been discussed, C.J.S. stands for Corpus Juris Secundum, the English translation from the Latin means "body of the law", and consists of several dozen large, dark blue volumes with gold lettering. Like the other law books West publishes, they come with an extensive index and annually updated pocket parts.

Step No. 7: Shepherd's Citators.

You will undoubtedly want to see similar cases and to make sure the case you are relying on has not been overturned. There are Shepherd's Citators for the Supreme Court, Federal Reporters, and Federal Supplements by number, by case, and by statute. Supplements to Shepherd's Citators are published every two months to keep abreast of changes in the law and new court cases. In front of each volume is an explanation of the abbreviations used in the body of the book. The abbreviations used refer to the history of the case and look like this:

a (affirmed) Same case affirmed on appeal
cc (connected case) Different case from case cited but arising out of same subject matter or intimately connected therewith.
r (reversed) Same case reversed on appeal
s (same case) Same case as case cited

Other abbreviations refer to the treatment of the case and look like this:

d (distinguished) Case at bar different either in law or fact from case cited for reasons given.
h (harmonized) Apparent inconsistency explained and shown not to exist.

There is also a Shepherd's referring to cases by name and allowing you to trace them down the same way. In such a book you find the *Miranda* and *Gideon* decisions.

On each page—upper left for left-hand pages, upper right for right-hand pages—of the Shepherd's using only case number references the volume number of the Reports or Reporter (and court) is listed. In 321 F.Supp. 1074 the 321 is on the upper left and

—1074—

is found in the middle of the page. Under —1074— are listed similar cases:

—1074—

a 407 US 297 United States (Supreme Court) Reports
a 32 L [2 752 Lawyer's Edition, (Supreme Court), Second Series
a 92 SC 2125 Supreme Court Reporter
442 F 2d 785 Federal Reporter, 2nd Series
486 F 2d16 966 Federal Reporter, 2nd Series
494 F 2d5 602 Federal Reporter, 2nd Series

The definitions on the right are not found in Shepherd's Citators. I merely put them in there for convenience.

The small numbers that look like an exponent for math simply tell you that key number is the only thing in the case that has any bearing on 321 F.Supp. 1074. The rest of the case is irrelevant for your purposes on that case.

Each key number in the Reporter(s) is developed more fully in the text of the opinion. Simply match the key numbers with the brackets [ ] in the same opinion.

Shepherd's also publishes citators for individual States. They work the same way as the Federal citators.

The easiest and most comprehensive way to deal with Shepherd's and a legal problem is to find a Supreme Court case "in point", i.e., similar to yours, and go from there. Cases abound in both U.S.C.A. and C.J.S. Once you have such a case, read and understand it thoroughly, and then pull the Supreme Court Citator, the one listed by number. In addition to all corresponding Supreme Court, Federal Appeals Court, and Federal District Court decisions there will be a list of all similar State decisions; since all Supreme Court decisions are binding on the states. Other Federal court decisions are not binding on the states unless they are addressed to a particular problem, such as prison overcrowding. In fact, Federal Appeals Court decisions in Chicago are not recognized, other than as a convenience, by District Courts outside of the Seventh Circuit.

A couple words of caution are in order here.

The first is that, during the years I spent in prison, I noticed most "jailhouse lawyers" only read parts of opinions that they THOUGHT were in their favor, ignoring everything —in the same opinion—that told them they had no chance. Read all opinions as if you were the OTHER side and you won't get into situations where you're defeated before you start.

The second is that if you get a "not to be published" opinion back on an appeal (the Seventh Circuit is famous for this) it means that—legally—you won but they just aren't going to let you have it. Sort of the legal language replacing the upraised fore finger gesture.

One of these days I hope to publish a series of law books titled "Unpublished Opinions"—as long as secret decisions are going to be made by dishonorable personalities (the law, the Constitution, and the taxpayer be damned) the rest of us at least ought to have a handy reference tool to be able to determine the types and personalities of the maniacs we're asking for "justice".

And if you run into words like "infra" meaning before, "supra" meaning after, "seriatim" meaning the answer in the same order you put the question, in a legal document, don't give up. Every decently-equipped law library has a "Black's Law Dictionary" that will tell you what the words mean. It's what the lawyers use when they don't understand each other.

5. Who Made The Rules?

You shouldn't even have to ask.

Lawyers, of course.

Lawyers in the House of Representatives and the Senate.

Not only have they drowned the rest of us with rules and laws that it takes a computer to contend with, they have created government bureaucracies by the score that pass "government regulations" in such tonnage (about 60,000 pages a year) that no American citizen can get through a day's work without violating a half dozen of them.

Why don't they repeal some of the laws?

Because—quite simply—any law, no matter how ridiculous, will keep lawyers employed. One of the worst was the 1968 Gun Control Act. It was passed right after Bobby Kennedy and Martin Luther King were gunned down. Hundreds of men have gone to prison because of that law.

The 1968 Gun Control Act is not only a bad law, it is a patently ridiculous and unconstitutional law.

Here's why:

I. The Constitution

"A well regulated Militia, being necessary to the security of a free State, the right of the people to keep and bear arms shall not be infringed."

—*Second Amendment, U.S. Constitution*

"Militia" according to the definition in use at the time the Constitution was written meant simply "armed citizens," consonant with Numbers 1:2-4 which is discussed further on. See definition in any 1828 Noah Webster dictionary. Hence the phrase "of the people," since the only difference between "Militia" and "people" in that day was one of armament, not enlistment.

Congress had no authority to pass the 1968 Gun Control Act since power not given to Congress was specifically reserved for the States—Amendment 10, U.S. Constitution, e.g., *Presser* v *Illinois* 116 U.S. 252, 265 (1886), and *United States* v *Cruikshank* 92 U.S. 542, 553 (1876).

The Supreme Court controlling case on a convicted felon possessing a firearm is *Scarborough* v *United States* ____U.S. ____, 52 L Ed 582, 97 S Ct ____, which, though it appears to preclude almost any hope for a defendant, only addresses the statutory construction of the statute and does not pass upon the constitutionality of the Act itself.

II. The Constitution and the Bible

The First Amendment makes it quite plain that Congress shall make no law prohibiting the exercise of religion. No religion can be sponsored or favored, none commanded, and none inhibited, *Walz* v *Tax Commissioner of City of New York* 397 U.S. 664, 694-697. Yet that is precisely what the Congress did with the act:

The Quakers, Jehovah's Witnesses, and a few other sects are not compelled to serve in our nation's armed forces since it is "against their religion". The Congress, under 18 USC app 1201 (3), makes the allegation that the possession of firearms by felons constitutes a ban to the "free exercise of religion". On the contrary, the free exercise of religion is severely and drastically curtailed by this Act for groups other than the Quakers, etc. for the following reasons:

1. Jesus Christ Himself would not be allowed to own a firearm — for He was a convicted felon (Mark 15:28, Isaiah 53:12). His teachings have been rendered wholly nugatory by the Congress, for it was He who said, "He who has no sword, let him sell his cloak and buy one."

Many religious groups believe Old Testament Law to be still in effect (Matthew 5:17-19).

Stemming from that same belief, all adult males over the age of 20 must be able to go to war (Numbers 1:2-4).

Those individuals must be taught archery (II Samuel 1:17-18). The word "archery" can, in the Herbrew, also be read "marksmanship", and it is obvious that God never intended His people to encumber themselves with swords and bows when pistols and rifles were available—the sword and the bow were simply the common infantry weapons used in His time on earth. To illustrate by way of similarities in the Bible, Ezekial I is an excellent description of a jet airplane but Ezekial calls it a "chariot".

2. According to many Biblical scholars' interpretation of Ezekial 38 and 39, the Russian Army is to invade the United States. Part of our "free exercise of religion" constitutes stockpiling weapons and ammunition for that event.

3. Which means a man whose only intention is to be faithful to the teachings of the Bible (e.g., "a strong man armed keepeth his house in peace"), should he be a convicted felon, is denied *his* freedom of religion by the Gun Control Act.

III. The Bible

The Bible itself is replete with the use of weapons by the "good guys". There is no provision in the Scriptures for disarming a class of people. However, there are numerous examples of what happens when the "rulers" are allowed to do so—in I Samuel the common man couldn't even get a tool sharpened unless he went down to the Philistines. Needless to say, the entire nation was reduced to slavery.

David did not slay Goliath with an Act of Congress.

"I come not to send peace, but a sword." (Matthew 10:34.)

One of the elements of proof to convict someone of a violation of the 1968 Gun Control Act required by the government is that a gun has traveled "in interstate commerce". Were his guns and the ammunition for them manufactured in his own state and never left the government's burden of proof becomes well-nigh impossible. It is quite possible some enterprising fellow will set up small gun manufacturing plants in each of the fifty states and sell guns to convicted felons that have not "traveled in interstate commerce".

The Act itself is almost comical in its twisting and distorting of even the most common rules of logic. 18 USC App 1201 (1) through (4) is quoted verbatim with the logical fallacies enumerated in parenthesis:

"The Congress hereby finds and declares that the receipt, possession, or transportation of a firearm by felons, veterans who are discharged under dishonarable conditions, mental incompetents, aliens who are illegally in the country, and former citizens who have renounced their citizenship, constitutes—

(my illustrations are only for convicted felons)

(1) a burden on commerce or threat affecting the free flow of commerce,

(How? Allegations unsupported by any line of reasoning are an automatic "F" in any high school composition class. This is a logical fallacy known as "poisoning the well").

(2) a threat to the safety of the President of the United States and the Vice President of the United States,

(Insufficient data to support the hypothesis. Of four successful presidential assassinations in the past two hundred years, how many were convicted felons? Bureau of Census records reveal that approximately twenty per cent of the adult population of the United States have sustained felony convictions. Does anyone really believe all those income tax evaders are bound and determined to kill Ronald Reagan?).

(3) an impediment or a threat to the exercise of free speech and the exercise of a religion guaranteed by the first amendment to the Constitution of the United States, and

(already discussed)

(4) a threat to the continued and effective operation of the Government of the United States and of the government of each State guaranteed by article IV of the Constitution.

Of course, the Government did not balk at giving convicted felons guns in WW II and allowing them their use in the armed forces when the government's continued and effective operation depended upon avenging Pearl Harbor. Either this paragraph seems to be a tacit admission that Congress knows "rehabilitation" does not work or a criminal conviction automatically turns every income tax evader into a demented trigger-happy lunatic bent on the destruction of all forms of government, including the state divorce courts mentioned in article IV. A logical fallacy known as hypothesis contrary to fact.

What type of experience did the lawyers in Congress have for passing a law disarming a large segment of the population, even if that law wasn't as absurd as it sounds?

In a word, none.

If you think living in a disarmed society can be peaceful and quiet read what this man has to say before you try to cram your views down the rest of our throats:

IN THE JUNGLE

The neighborhood I live in, judged in accordance with the "facts" the gun control fans would have us believe, should be absolutely perfect. It is located in what appears to be, on the surface, a pleasant rural area with a large river close by and most of the land in cultivation or utilized for pasture for cattle and hogs. There is a large industry here that employs several hundred people and while the wages are not the highest no-one is starving and anyone in the neighborhood who wants to work, can. We have no unemployment problem and those that want to can pursue a higher education. There is no pollution. It is a small community, with only a few blocks, a hospital, one store, a gym, and a cafeteria. It is approximately 50% black, 40% white, and 10% Spanish descent—a completely integrated society. The population total is less than 1300 and the area most of us live in comprises about 28 acres. According to most studies put out by government planners, pointing out the reasons for crime and violence (lack of employment opportunities, higher education, and food) one would think our little community would be a veritable Utopia. Except for one minor detail.

There is one major drawback to living in this idyllic little community. No-one here, including the police, are allowed any type of a firearm or other weapon. The police, possibly because of the fact that they are not allowed any sort of weapon, travel in huge numbers to quell any sort of disturbance at a tremendous cost to the taxpayers. They can hardly be blamed for operating in such a fashion because it is the only way they have of protecting themselves from injury. Unfortunately, the "protect oneself" mentality has serious side effects upon the citizenry. If a citizen commits an offense the police simply lock him up, no matter how serious it is. On the other hand, if a common man attacks one of the minions of the law the response is usually to beat the offender into a vegetable. Because of the extremely large numbers of police necessary to keep order in a weaponless society citizen/police friction stays at a maximum ("they seem to be constantly underfoot or bossing people around") and a citizen who normally would take a poke at an overbearing officer winds up venting his hostility on another citizen. He, after all, does not want to be beaten into a vegetable. The situation is further complicated in that, since the police are so vulnerable themselves, they are simply not interested in setting up any kind of a situation where the population might turn on them—so as long as the citizens stab and club each other they, at most, get locked up for a few months—and six weeks is about average.

Some of the more enterprising have learned how to cope with "police indifference." Unfortunately, the ones who learn how to cope are usually the most cunning and dangerous themselves. A recent case in point: the police received information that the Moors, a militant black religious group, was going to stir up trouble because of the large amount of pork in the local diet. The police got their information from several different informers in different parts of the neighborhood and figured it had to be reliable. Since a large-scale riot might involve police getting hurt they had to move quickly—and those movements, in a society where the Second Amendment to the U.S. Constitution does not exist, are not hampered by such political inconveniences as due process and unreasonable search and seizure. As many now-extinct societies found out at their demise, once the right to own weapons vanishes, so do all other rights except those of the privileged elite. The religious leaders were swooped down on and locked up within a matter of hours.

Quite some time later, after several people had been deported from the nieghborhood, it was learned that the Moors had been the victims of a rather devious ploy by a group of white dope dealers who wanted them out of the way. What the dope dealers had done was to let various informers "overhear" various snatches of conversation, the informers ran to the police with it, and the unarmed police reacted in the only predictable way they could to prevent a situation that—had it been real—they either could not have controlled or sustained numerous and serious injuries within their own ranks.

One of the main bars to acquiring firearms in my neighborhood is that the penalities for their possession and use are too severe. Both the seller and the purchaser can receive up to ten years in prison for so much as dealing in a single bullet. Shoot someone with that single bullet and the fellow who pulled the trigger—no matter what the circumstances—faces another 99 years. Nor are crooked police interested in dealing in guns. The narcotics trade here is far more lucrative. And safer.

The lack of guns does not deter the cunning and predatory types from acquiring weapons, however. Even though any weapon is illegal here making knives and clubs is a simple matter, and those who intend to "break the rules" anyway are not going to be deterred by the possibility of being locked up for a week because they had a lethal weapon in their possession.

Contrary to what the gun control advocates would have folks believe, eliminating guns does not eliminate crime—on the contrary, it increases it. Narcotics transactions of large magnitude "go down" almost daily in my neighborhood, robbery (both armed and burglary) is an every other day occurrence, and serious assaults with pipes or knives, sometimes resulting in murder, run as high as a dozen a month.

In any given year we have over forty (40) stabbings in this neighborhood. Some are fatal. Since 1972, 174 men have died of stab wounds in this community. Considering there are less than 1300 people living in the area at any one time simple arithmetic indicates the average person living here has a one in ten chance of leaving in a pine box in any given four-year period. Naturally, no life insurance company will write business here and time payment plans are non-existent.

The liberals are bound to come up with what appear to be very valid arguments for letting people carry knives instead of guns for self-protection. Those of us here, having been deprived of any guns we once had, know why knives and clubs don't do the job.

First, predators in an unarmed society travel the same way the police do — in packs. It is relatively easy for a half dozen men with knives and clubs to overcome one man armed similarly. Especially if he's trying to protect someone else.

Second, contrary to the nonsense shown in the movies, stabbing a man does not "drop" him at once—in many cases it doesn't even slow him down. Especially if he's scared or mad. I've seen it happen often enough to know. On the other hand, a .45 caliber pistol is usually quite effective at dropping unsociable types on the first round and it's not even necessary to hit a vital area.

Third, while it is relatively easy to surround someone with a knife or a club it is almost impossible to do so to a man with a barking pistol. What most folks don't realize is that a pistol is primarily a DEFENSIVE weapon—it is the "equalizer" for the woman home alone, the cripple in the wheelchair, the owner of the "Mom & Pop" Grocery, and the person outnumbered. Who comes out on top in a fight with knives or clubs usually depends on physical size and strength; sometimes skill. Yet a 16 year old girl with a 12 gauge shotgun and the ability and willingness to use it is, at a distance of ten feet, a match for almost any man on the face of the earth.

Here that same girl would probably be raped to death

within a matter of minutes. Rape and extortion seem to be our most commonly practiced criminal activities here, second only to dope dealing. The young and unsuspecting are often lured into situations by the gangs that run in the neighborhood, beaten (often with lead pipes), raped, and sometimes left for dead. In many cases the victim is "befriended", invited to some quiet and secluded spot to smoke a couple reefers, and when the victim realizes what his "friends" REALLY have in mind (around here, usually sodomy) it is too late to escape the trap. He's obviously not going to pull a handgun out of his pocket, is he? Occasionally the criminal gangs, if they are large enough, simply grab whoever they want and sodomize them in front of witnesses.

Extortion here is practiced either by threats of physical violence or sometimes merely by a gang barging into someone's house and taking what they want while the victim is held at bay by knifepoint. Obviously no gang with any collective sense is going to try such a stunt on a man armed with a revolver but when the robbers know the best weapon their victim can come up with is a knife, a pipe, or a broom handle the worst that can happen to them is they will simply have to back off and rob someone else.

Since narcotics flow so freely in this neighborhood rip-off artists and junkies looking for a prey are legion. I've seen men stabbed because they sold other men bags of sugar, passing it off as heroin. And men worked over with an ice-pick because they owed money. And men sliding around in pools of their own blood on the floor; trying to get away from their attackers and knowing that no-one will help them because they can't—they are unarmed. And homosexual rape victims revenge themselves on their violators by plunging knives into them while they sleep.

The tension here is unbelievable; the very air is permeated with it. The rule is, travel in a pack and watch your back. A lot of men join the gangs simply for self-protection—meaning three really evil individuals who might be contained wind up picking up a half dozen followers and become completely unstoppable.

"Set-ups" are common. An individual is told he is supposed to go somewhere or be someplace and the minute he turns the wrong corner he is set upon by a pack with knives. There are few less horrible ways to die than to be butchered while still breathing.

The neighborhood I live in is not a foreign country, it is located in the MidWestern United States. It is sometimes sarcastically referred to as The Gladiator School but its official designation is Terre Haute Federal Penitentiary, Terre Haute, Indiana.

The blocks I referred to earlier are cellblocks, the store is the prison commissary, the cafeteria is the prison mess hall, a "house" is prison slang for an individual cell, and the police are the prison guards.

It is really unfortunate that some of the anti-gun legislators and bleeding hearts don't have the benefit of living in my neighborhood—seeing a man run through from stomach to back with an 18" knife and then set upon by others who stab out his eyes does wonders for one's perspective concerning the possession of firearms.

Doesn't concern you because we're "just convicts" and we're locked up and can't do "society" any harm?

Guess again. The Federal Bureau of Prisons incarcerates four (4) blacks for every white — yet a Federal penitentiary such as this one very seldom gets over fifty per cent (50%) black. Why? Because the white prison administrators are no more capable of keeping a predominantly black population in line (remember, these are convicts, not members of the NAACP or the Urban League) than a handful of blacks would be able to run a prison full of Klansmen. So enough blacks are paroled to keep the "racial balance" even, the whites are forced to do all their time and come out extremely embittered and sometimes dangerous, some real lunatics are foisted upon society, and for what: so the prison officials and employees, who may not carry guns inside the compound, can work in safety.

The Constitution, including the Second Amendment, was written by men of vision and experience. I have had the "experience"—and I don't like it. Neither would you.

Then there are the government agencies and bureaucracies proliferating like rabbits.

It took an Act of Congress to create each and every one of such living abortions as HEW, HUD, OSHA, etc.

Why did the Congress foist these monsters on us?

In a word, irresponsibility.

The Congress is totally unwilling to regulate the federal judiciary and so here's what happens:

A big coal company dumps tons of coal slag into a river and ruins the water for everyone in an entire county — or series of counties.

Some young lawyer is hired by citizens whose water has been poisoned to do battle with the corporate giant and make it pay for its misdeeds.

The federal judge the case goes in front of airily dismisses the grievances of several hundred—or thousand—American citizens with a flip of his wrist. After all, he and the owner of the coal company are probably golfing buddies and members of the "elite" of society. The judge is impervious to judgment.

The enraged citizens then go to their Congressman and demand that he "do something".

Instead of instituting impeachment proceedings or passing a bill to control the judge the Congressman confers with other Congressmen, finds that a lot of them have constituents with the same complaint, and creates another monolithic federal agency to cope with it.

Like the E.P.A.

That is, because one or two federal judges play favorites, the taxpayers are now saddled with a multi-billion dollar agency to see to it that people don't have their drinking water polluted.

The only thing that changes is that in place of one young lawyer hired by private citizens the E.P.A. sends in droves of government drones, papershufflers, and lawyers.

Nothing gets done.

Except that several thousand more lawyers are now supported at the public trough.

6. Making A Judge Behave

It may initially seem strange to you that this chapter would appear before the one on laying the groundwork for a case and other subjects.

There's a logical explanation for this.

Once you learn the "ropes" in the federal system and get "blooded" a bit, litigation in any state court should be fairly uncomplicated. That is, the federal courts are so totally corrupt that mastering them is the legal equivalent of going 15 rounds—and winning—with the World Heavyweight Boxing Champion. Many state courts—in comparison—can't be considered a contest compared to the federal courts simply because your main adversary, by doing exactly what he's supposed to do, doesn't cause you any problems at all.

In federal court your main enemy is the judge.

Make no mistake about it.

Anyone acting as his own lawyer in federal court is going to spend 10% of his time fighting his LEGAL opponent—the plaintiff or defendant—and 90% of the time fighting the unlawful, arrogant, and one-sided behavior of the judge. There will be specific examples of this in later chapters.

In federal court, your opponent (defendant) is usually a federal employee, agency, or defendant residing in another state represented by an admitted member of the bar.

If you are representing yourself here is what usually happens:

1. You file a complaint against a federal bureacrat.

2. They have so many days to answer according to the Federal Rules of Civil Procedure. The judge normally orders them to answer accordingly within so many days.

3. The answer you get back from the defendant is normally full of meaningless doubletalk.

4. The next thing that happens to you or your complaint is one of two things:

a) The judge rules against you, regardless of the facts and the law in the case. This is normally the best you can hope for in federal court. At least it allows you to go to the Appeals Court.

b) If you have a good, solid, well-prepared case what USUALLY happens is the judge simply "sits" on it. Sort of like stopping the clock when the football team he likes is losing. As you can see by the following civil action it's also a practice readily engaged in by lesser bureacrats.

According to Acts of Congress—such as 28 USC 2243 in habeas corpus cases—they simply don't have the authority to pull such stunts.

In complaints against federal bureaucrats—especially prison personnel, FBI agents, and the like—the response is normally prepared by a United States Attorney.

At the local level, the "D.A."

That is, if you file a claim against a bureaucrat for criminal conduct, a civil action asking money damages, the man who is SUPPOSED to be putting evildoers behind bars—the United States Attorney—is the one assigned to DEFEND the criminal.

Here is a case in point (it was transferred from Ohio):

SAMPLE DOCUMENT

IN THE
UNITED STATES DISTRICT COURT
FOR THE SOUTHERN DISTRICT OF OHIO

HAROLD JAMES JENKS, Plaintiff v KATY LOUDERMILK P.R. ROLLINS, Defendants	))))))))	Civil Action No. _______ COMPLAINT

JURISDICTION

1. This action containing complaints for declaratory relief and for damages, is brought against the defendants to secure due process of law, equal protection and other rights, privileges and immunities guaranteed to complainant by the Constitution and laws of these United States.

2. Jurisdiction is invoked under the United States Code as follows:

A. 28 U.S.C. §1331 in that the matter in controversy exceeds the sum of $10,000, exclusive of interest and cost, and arises under the Constitution and laws of the United States.

B. 28 U.S.C.§ 1332 (a)(1) in that the action arises between citizens of different States.

C. 28 U.S.C. §1343

(1) To recover damages for injury to his person or property or because of the deprivation of any right or privilege of a citizen of the United States, by an act done in furtherance of any conspiracy mentioned in section 1985 of Title 42;

(This document is a facsimile which was re-typed to improve legibility. For a reproduction of the original document, turn to page 171.)

SAMPLE DOCUMENT

(2) To recover damages from any person who fails to prevent or to aid in preventing any wrongs mentioned in section 1985 of Title 42 which he had knowledge were about to occur and power to prevent;

(B) To recover damages or to secure equitable or other relief under any Act of Congress providing for the protection of civil rights, including the right to vote.

D. 28 U.S.C. § 2201 and 2202.

E. 42 U.S.C. § 1981.

F. 42 U.S.C. § 1985 and 1986.

G. All of the above statutes but not limited thereto.

VENUE

3. Venue for this action is proper under 28 U.S.C. § 1391(e)(4) in that the plaintiff has a residence of 717 Old Main Street, Miamisburg Ohio 45342 and 1037 Primrose Drive, West Carrollton, Ohio.

In determining domicile at common law, a change from one domicile to another requires proof. Together with physical removal of a person, there must be an accompanying intent to change domicile. Otherwise, the body will have moved, but the domicile will have remained where it was next in time prior thereto.

Ballas v Symm 351 F. Supp. 876, 886

There was no voluntary intent to change domicile by the plaintiff as he is a Federal prisoner:

Venue of action by federal prisoner was proper in district wherein petitioner was domiciled before his incarceration.

United States ex rel Harrison v Pace
357 F. Supp. 354

In action by federal prisoner against parole board seeking mandamus, venue was present under 28 U.S.C. § 1391(e) in district of prisoner's residence, even though prisoner was then incarcerated in different district.

Stone v United States Board of Parole
360 F. Supp. 22

Both defendants are Federal employees and the emphasis on venue under 28 U.S.C. § 1391(e)(4) should be readily self-evident upon a complete reading of the complaint.

SAMPLE DOCUMENT

PLAINTIFF

4. Plaintiff HAROLD JAMES JENKS is and was at all times mentioned herein a prisoner in custody of the United States Bureau of Prisons. He is currently confined in the United States Penitentiary, Terre Haute, Indiana.

DEFENDANTS

5. Katy Loudermilk is the Clerk of the Court for the Terre Haute Division of the United States District Court for the Southern District of Indiana.

6. P.R. Rollins was the caseworker assigned to the plaintiff during the time the incidents enumerated took place. He is currently employed in the Drug Abuse Program at Terre Haute penitentiary.

FACTS

7. In June 1976 the plaintiff's attorney, Mr. F. Dane Delcontivo, mailed via certified mail two (2) petitions to the United States District Court from Dayton, Ohio. At the same time a check was mailed in the amount of $30.00 (thirty dollars) to insure prompt service on both petitions.

8. A few days after the petitions were mailed from Dayton the plaintiff walked into defendant ROLLINS' office and the defendant was holding a telephone conversation. He (Rollins) did not notice the plaintiff standing in front of him. Defendant ROLLINS was writing something on a paper on his desk and talking to defendant LOUDERMILK on the telephone. The two defendants were discussing the mandamus petition the plaintiff had filed.

Defendant ROLLINS then looked up and saw the plaintiff standing in front of him. He turned white as if all the blood had drained from his face.

SAMPLE DOCUMENT

The plaintiff then inquired if defendant ROLLINS was talking to defendant LOUDERMILK about his case. Defendant ROLLINS sputtered and stammered and finally informed the plaintiff that defendant LOUDERMILK had called him and wanted to talk to the plaintiff. The plaintiff told defendant ROLLINS he was not allowed to discuss the plaintiff's petitions with the court clerk.

Defendant ROLLINS then hung up the telephone and refused to talk to the plaintiff.

One of the items overheard by the plaintiff said by defendant ROLLINS was, "Give me some time".

9. The mandamus petition filed in Terre Haute was to force the defendant ROLLINS to answer an Administrative Remedy Form (BP-9) that was out of time and the plaintiff had, before the mandamus action was filed, been informed by defendant ROLLINS that the BP-9 would not be answered.

10. Several days later, after the telephone call mentioned in (8), the plaintiff was summoned to the counselor's office and handed the BP-9 in litigation (the object of the mandamus) with an answer on it. The plaintiff asked his counselor, Mr. Barnett, why the BP-9 was finally answered several days out of time. Mr. Barnett informed the plaintiff that he did not know since he (Mr. Barnett) was also informed that the plaintiff would not receive an answer to his BP-9. The plaintiff then informed Mr. Barnett of the telephone call between defendants ROLLINS and LOUDERMILK. Mr. Barnett merely shrugged his shoulders and refused to comment further.

SAMPLE DOCUMENT

11. Several days later the plaintiff inquired of his attorney what the docket numbers on the two petitions were. He did not know and was under the impression the docket numbers and receipt for filing fee had been forwarded to the plaintiff from the District Court in Terre Haute. At this time the plaintiff's attorney was unaware of the telephone call between defendants ROLLINS and LOUDERMILK.

12. The next time the plaintiff talked to his attorney he was informed that the attorney had called the court and talked to Mrs. Loudermilk, was given the run-around, the petitions had not been filed, there were no docket numbers, his $30.00 check was returned, and she kept the petitions.

13. A week later the plaintiff again walked into defendant ROLLINS' office and again he was talking to defendant LOUDERMILK on the telephone. Defendant ROLLINS then handed the telephone to the plaintiff. Defendant LOUDERMILK then informed the plaintiff that she had just called to "explain to you what you have to do to get a docket number."

14. The plaintiff's girlfriend and her room-mate telephoned defendant LOUDERMILK, got nasty about it, and in November, 1976, five months after the plaintiff tried to file his petitions, he received a docket number. One of the petitions had to be withdrawn since it was a FREEDOM OF INFORMATION ACT action that became mooted by the actions of defendant LOUDERMILK.

15. It took the plaintiff's attorney, Mrs. Sandy Egelston, Mrs. Carolyn Sue Hall, and the plaintiff through their combined efforts from July 1976 until November 1976 to get defendant LOUDERMILK to file one (1) petition.

SAMPLE DOCUMENT

LEGAL CLAIMS

16. The plaintiff, an American citizen, has an unqualified Constitutional right to access to the courts. The actions of the defendants not only precluded the plaintiff's lawful access to the Courts and denied him due process of law but were in addition felonies under Title 18, United States Code:

18 U.S.C. § 2 Whoever commits an offense against the United States or aids, abets, counsels, commands, induces or procures its commission, is punishable as a principal.

18 U.S.C. § 4 Misprision of a felony.

18 U.S.C. § 241 Conspiracy against rights of citizens.

18 U.S.C. § 371 Conspiracy to commit offense or to defraud United States.

18 U.S.C. § 401(2) Misbehavior of court officers in their official transactions.

18 U.S.C. § 1001 Lying and covering up.

18 U.S.C. § 1505 Obstruction of justice.

18 U.S.C. § 1905 Disclosure of confidential information.

And as of Sept. 28, 1976 no court clerk may refuse a petition. Public Law 94-426.

RELIEF REQUESTED

1. A declaratory judgment that the defendants' acts, policies, and practices described herein violate plaintiff's rights under the United States Constitution.

2. Compensatory damages in the amount of $50,000 from each defendant.

3. Punitive damages in the amount of $50,000 from each defendant.

4. Jury trial on all issues triable by jury.

5. Plaintiff's cost of this suit.

SAMPLE DOCUMENT

6. An Order removing both defendants LOUDERMILK and ROLLINS from Government employment consonant with 18 U.S.C. § 1905 which provides in part: "...and shall be removed from office or employment."

7. Such other relief as this Court deems just, proper, and equitable.

Respectfully Submitted,

____
HAROLD JAMES JENKS
Reg. No. 30636-117
P.O. Box 33
Terre Haute, Indiana 47808

Subscribed and Sworn to
before me this ____ day
of February, 1977.

____
UNITED STATES PAROLE OFFICER

SAMPLE DOCUMENT

IN THE
UNITED STATES DISTRICT COURT
FOR THE SOUTHERN DISTRICT OF INDIANA
TERRE HAUTE DIVISION

HAROLD JAMES JENKS, MICHAEL H. BROWN, Plaintiffs v KATY LOUDERMILK, P.R. ROLLINS J.B. JOHNSON, J.W. JEAN, Defendants	)	Civil Action No. TH-77-54-C

AMENDMENT TO COMPLAINT

Come the plaintiffs in the above numbered cause, HAROLD JAMES JENKS and MICHAEL H. BROWN, and amend and supplement this complaint in accordance with Federal Rules of Civil Procedure 15(a)(c), 19(a)(1) - (2) and 20(a).

1. MICHAEL H. BROWN Reg. No. 81856, incarcerated at Terre Haute Prison, Terre Haute, Indiana 47808 is added as a plaintiff for any and several of the following reasons:

A. On March 23, 1976 defendant LOUDERMILK jeopardized and interfered with the legal and civil rights of plaintiff BROWN by unauthorized disclosure of information and other illegal acts enumerated in the original complaint (Appendix A) and in addition caused the plaintiff great mental distress.

B. On July 27, 1976 defendant LOUDERMILK failed to record a MOTION TO ISSUE SHOW CAUSE ORDER submitted by plaintiff BROWN in violation of the Federal statutes mentioned in the original complaint. The plaintiff has a copy in his possession of said MOTION stamped "filed" by the U.S. District Court, Terre Haute, and said motion does not appear on the docket sheet prepared by defendant LOUDERMILK.

C. Defendant LOUDERMILK refused to schedule plaintiff BROWN's habeas corpus petition, TH-76-88-C, in accordance with 28 U.S.C.§ 2243 and Federal Rule of Civil Procedure 81(a)(2), causing plaintiff BROWN to take from June 15 to November 23, 1976 to get a hearing on his petition.

D. From information and belief defendant LOUDERMILK telephoned the Terre Haute prison and through her unlawful influence caused the ruling on said habeas corpus petition issued by the Court and all other legal and personal mail belonging to the plaintiff to be mis-routed to a Community Treatment Center (Talbott House) in Ohio in order to prevent plaintiff BROWN from prosecuting an appeal on said habeas corpus petition --- a situation remedied only by the due diligence of plaintiff BROWN.

E. On Dec. 8, 1976 plaintiff BROWN wrote defendant LOUDERMILK as to the status of his court proceedings. In consequence plaintiff BROWN was summoned to the counselor's office at 3:05 p.m. December 14, 1976 and before leaving at 3:40 p.m. that date threatened with "disciplinary action" by hereinafter named defendant J.W. Jean if he (BROWN) wrote any more letters to defendant LOUDERMILK.

3. For the reasons given in 2(E) J.W. Jean is added as a defendant.

4. For the following reasons J.B. Johnson is added as a defendant:

A. In August or early September 1976 plaintiff JENKS walked into defendant JOHNSON's office and found said defendant on the telephone conversing with defendant LOUDERMILK. Defendant JOHNSON immediately handed plaintiff JENKS the telephone. Plaintiff JENKS than inquired of defendant LOUDERMILK the reason(s) he had not received a reply to his correspondence requesting a docket number. Defendant LOUDERMILK replied that she had sent the plaintiff JENKS "several letters" detailing

SAMPLE DOCUMENT

the problem. Plaintiff JENKS NEVER received any such letters nor were any to be found in his central file.

B. Judging from the foregoing it appears that J.B. JOHNSON and J.W. JEAN had joined in as willing co-conspirators.

Wherefore, the plaintiffs request this Court permit the foregoing amendment and supplementation to the original complaint and in addition:

1. That the Court order the defendants to retain their own personal counsel since the acts described in this complaint are not part of their jobs and

2. This Court prohibit the defendants, their employees, or associates from initiating retaliatory action against the plaintiffs for the filing of this action; such actions (usually) taking the form of "administrative" transfers, job changes, or other subtle forms of harrassment.

Subscribed and Sworn to
before me this _____ day
of May, 1977.

Respectfully Submitted,

UNITED STATES PAROLE OFFICER

HAROLD JAMES JENKS
Reg. No. 30636 - 117

UNITED STATES PAROLE OFFICER

MICHAEL H. BROWN
Reg. No. 81856 - 158

P.O. Box 33
Terre Haute, Indiana 47808

SAMPLE DOCUMENT

M.H. Brown
Reg. No. 81856
P.O. Box 33
Terre Haute, Indiana
March 9, 1976

Dear Sirs,

Would you please send Harold Smith 30912-138(G), P.O. Box 33, Terre Haute, Indiana, the necessary Habeas Corpus forms pursuant to Local Rule 25?

He is in "administration segregation" for "convenience of the administration" reasons and I intend to file a "next friend" Habeas Corpus for him.

Thank You,

Michael H. Brown

3/23/76

Dear Mr. Johnston:

Pursuant to telephone conversation this date with a member of your staff, I am returning herewith the letter received in this. Thank you very much.

Deputy Clerk
(Katy Loudermilk)

You can also report this type of criminal misbehavior to the FBI but it doesn't do any good. On the following pages you'll find what happened when we did:

SAMPLE DOCUMENT

Harold James Jenks
Reg. No. 30636-117
P.O. Box 33
Terre Haute, Indiana
47808

Mr. Neil Smiley,

Just a note to let you know how things are going with me since I had my talk with you and also to ask you a question or two.

First of all I should let you know I am now paying the price for going to you for help.

When I left you a few weeks ago I went to see my team. You will find how I fared in the appendixes attached to this letter. Since that time I have talked to Mr. Wally Buer in the hallway of the C&P and tried to find out why such strong statements were made against me. Mr. Buer would not talk to me except to say that he knew what I was trying to do and that I was not going to get away with it.

There are only two things he can be talking about. The first one is my legal work which they have been aware of for the past 14 mo., and two, the fact that I went to the F.B.I. for help.

My caseworker Mr. J.B. Johnson has never at any time in all the meetings I have had with him mentioned any of the things my team has used against me in the context they were used.

The questions I must ask you are (1) did you have a conversation with the staff, "in particular Mr. Wally Buer" earlier in the day you talked to me? (2) Have you had to talk with any of the staff about me since then? I have seen you in the hall corrider 6 times so far and remember seeing you before I knew who you were. You must come up here a lot?

I am sorry to take up your time but I would like you to read my progress Report. The first 3 pages were done by my caseworker before I talked to you. Page 4 was done by my casemanagement team

(This document is a facsimile which was re-typed to improve legibility. For a reproduction of the original document, turn to page 182.)

after I talked to you. The team is headed by Mr. Wally Buer.

The other letter is what I wrote to the Parole Board. I think the two are self explanatory. I go in front of the Parole Board the second week in June for my 13 hearing. What do you think my chances are NOW?

I would also like to know the name and address of the District Attorney you are talking to.

MORE GOOD NEWS: The original writ that Mrs. Loudermilk refused to docket in June, 1976, and the subsequent phone calls to Mr. Rollins allowed them to answer the B.P.9 they refused to answer, and were out of time before she finally gave me a docket number in December 1976.

I have just received a denial from Judge Dillin on my custody writ. The reason for denial was that I have not exhausted my administrative remedies. Mrs. Loudermilk's interference was directly responsible for this ruling. So far it has cost me a year's delay and looking forward to another year delay in the Appeals Court, along with all the money, effort, and time involved.

Request Response As Soon As Possible.

Thank You,

cc: Mr. Hargraves

Mr. Harold James Jenks

At the time this was written Neil Smiley was the FBI agent (supposedly) covering the affairs at the prison. He could normally be seen laughing and drinking coffee with the prison personnel while I was there. As far as I know he never actually investigated anything, even when we were having a dozen stabbings a month.

It might, at this point, be wise to explain what federal "law enforcement" agencies actually do so you don't wind up in the same trap we did.

The average government "law officer" is not interested in preventing crime or apprehending criminals. They can't. They're too clumsy.

What they actually do is CREATE crimes (such as (Abscam) in order to then "catch" the "criminals" and get favorable media attention in order to insure they don't get their budgets cut at the next session of Congress.

One of the worst offenders is the Secret Service. In one case I know of, they made a deal with a 6'6", 450 lb. child molester (22 counts, including rape on a 14 year old girl) to get the State of Ohio charges off of him and relocate him under the "witness protection program" in exchange for his talking someone else into becoming involved in counterfeiting. While the "set-up" was going on the Secret Service was financing him in a narcotics operation to keep him financially afloat (they never arrested anyone for narcotics nor reported such dealings to the State or Federal drug agents).

Your tax dollars at work.

To keep a jury from getting suspicious such people are never sentenced until AFTER their victim is put away. Who would believe someone who got probation on 22 counts of child molesting didn't "squeal for a deal" or wasn't a PAID prosecution witness?

I found this out the hard way. Two snitches who gave me up in 1974 swore up and down under oath that they had made "no deals" to rat on me. This was AFTER a state judge had told them he was going to "throw the book at them" for burglarizing a W.T. Grant store in that city.

After a few conversations with FBI agent John Gill (Lexington) and a lot of perjured testimony what they got was probation. In the documental illustration of the Stafford sentencing, "good behavior" simply means squealing.

SAMPLE DOCUMENT

C 750390

003 DT 75.085 10.10
DY*
PD RICHMOND
LARRY AND WM STAFFORD INDICTED 072574 PLEAD GUILTY ON 022575
CIRCUIT CT ON AMENDED CHARGE OF ATT TO COMMIT A FELONY GIVEN ONE
YR CO JAIL SUSPENDED SENTENCE FOR 1 YR GOOD BEHAVIOR
PD FKFT DJD

About the only way you can cope with this type of government misconduct is to put heat on the judge (even though it's not his fault in THIS case) and file every motion available to try to stall the action until AFTER the rat (or rats, as the case may be) in the case has been sentenced. And sent to prison. Then all you have to do is hope you don't get eaten cheese on for a parole.

Unfortunately, there is a large body of case law to the effect that you can't sue someone for perjured testimony in a criminal prosecution—at least in federal court. Of course, you could go to the FBI. That is, if you believe in the tooth fairy, Santa Claus, and government agents making a good faith investigation of perjury they coached stool pigeons to commit.

Which brings us full circle to my original point—making a judge behave.

It's not easy.

The law books list only two ways. Which is all we will cover in this chapter.

One is called a Writ of Mandamus.

The other is called a Writ of Prohibition.

Most attorneys avoid them like the plague even if it means seeing their client flushed down the drain. Makes the judges mad—something toadying attorneys can't handle.

As you may know, a federal or state judge cannot be sued for anything he does in his official capacity, no matter how outrageous or unprincipled. This was not a gift given to them by Congress, they just overstepped the bounds of their authority (as usual) and gave it to themselves.

To make a judge do what he was supposed to do in the first place you file a petition for a Writ of Mandamus (mandamus, "we command") in the next higher court. A lot of jailhouse lawyers are referred to as "writ writers" but that's a misnomer—only a judge can issue a writ.

For example, if a federal judge in a District Court is dragging his feet on a case you simply file a petition in the appropriate Court of Appeals asking them to make him get off his butt. The judges in the Southern District of Indiana are notorious for this in habeas corpus cases. My experience here has been that it will never be issued but it does have two other salutary effects:

1. It makes the judge look like a jerk to the judges higher up.

2. It makes him issue a ruling almost at once. Of course, it will be against you but he was going to rule against you anyway. All this does is get you to the Appeals Court fourteen months earlier.

The reason the judge rules so fast is that the U.S. Attorney is not allowed to defend him. He has to hire his own lawyer. Of course, it costs you $50.00 to file it but—if it's done right—it can cause the judge $5000 worth of headaches. On a $60,000 a year salary (before taxes) you only have to "score" once or twice to cause him serious financial problems.

What happens is they always make a move to moot the action before they have to mount a defense. You can only do damage to him if he a) can't move or b) is just obstinate.

In Terre Haute—when I wanted a judge to move—I finally learned that all I had to do was send the judge a certified copy of the petition for Writ of Mandamus (which you have to do anyway). My victim would always move to moot it within a week to ten days so I wouldn't be able to tie him up in the Appeals Court. I never had to pay the $50.00 since I never actually filed any of them.

A friend of mine in Terre Haute came up with one where we could have tied the judge up in court and cost him a fortune. Unfortunately, my friend filed a Motion to Proceed In Forma Pauperis (no $50.00; at taxpayer's expense) and the Seventh Circuit Court of Appeals dismissed it as "frivolous".

They do that when you try for a free ride.

The other little judicial behavioral tool is known as a Writ of Prohibition. The only difference between this one and Mandamus is that here you want the judge to STOP doing something. This case (a free one described in preceeding paragraph — it worked) was typical:

SAMPLE DOCUMENT

UNITED STATES COURT OF APPEALS
FOR THE SEVENTH CIRCUIT

HAROLD JAMES JENKS, MICHAEL H. BROWN, Plaintiffs v CALE J. HOLDER, Defendant	))))))))	Civil Action No. PETITION FOR WRIT OF PROHIBITION

JURISDICTION

Jurisdiction of this court is invoked under 28 USC 1651.

PARTIES

The plaintiffs are federal prisoners incarcerated at Terre Haute federal prison, Terre Haute, Indiana.

The defendant is a federal judge in charge of the Terre Haute division of the Southern District of Indiana.

FACTS

1. The plaintiffs are scheduled for trial on December 22, 1977 9 a.m. at the Terre Haute courthouse by order of the defendant.

2. The defendant, it appears, has scheduled all Terre Haute prisoner complaints, including jury trials, for December 22, as he has done for a number of years.

3. The complaint scheduled for trial is one against the defendant's court clerk, Katy Loudermilk, docket number TH 77-54-C.

4. Based on (3), the defendants filed an affidavit of bias and prejudice against Judge Holder according to the provisions of 28 USC 144.

(This document is a facsimile which was re-typed to improve legibility.
For a reproduction of the original document, turn to page 184.)

SAMPLE DOCUMENT

5. Based on past experience (see e.g. Brown v Williams 77-1228) the plaintiffs have no reason to believe that Judge Holder can conduct himself lawfully regarding the rights of prisoners: any judge who can schedule several "jury trials" with himself as presiding judge is in no way qualified to arbitrate fairly between the parties.

LEGAL CLAIMS

6. The three elements necessary for prohibition are present in the instant case:

A. That the person it is directed against is about to exercise judicial power.

B. That the exercise of such power by said person is unauthorized by law.

C. That it will result in injury for which there is no other adequate remedy.

7. The minute Judge Holder received the affidavit of bias and prejudice he lost jurisdiction over TH 77-54-C.

8. It is patently illegal for a judge to orchestrate several trials on the same day and at the same time; a courtroom is not a TV set where the viewer can change channels if he gets bored.

Subscribed and sworn to
before me this ____ day
of December, 1977.

Respectfully Submitted,

____
UNITED STATES PAROLE OFFICER

____
Harold James Jenks
Reg No 30636-117

____
UNITED STATES PAROLE OFFICER

____
Michael H. Brown
Reg No 81856-158

Authorized by the Act of July 7, 1955
to administer oaths (18 U.S.C. 4004)

P.O. Box 33
Terre Haute, Indiana 47808

SAMPLE DOCUMENT

CERTIFICATE OF SERVICE

This is to certify that I have on this ____ day of December, 1977 placed a true and exact copy of the foregoing in the U.S. Mails addressed to Hon Cale J Holder, U.S. District Court, Southern District of Indiana, Terre Haute Division, Terre Haute, Indiana 47808.

____
Harold James Jenks

Again, never granted.

If you think I'm kidding, look who asked for THIS Writ of Mandamus: Frederick M. Coleman, U.S. Atty., N. D. Ohio, Cleveland, Ohio, Henry E. Petersen, Asst. Atty. Gen., Crim. Div., Dept. of Justice, Washington D.C., for petitioner.

UNITED STATES v. BATTISTI
cite as 486 F.2d 961 (1973)

UNITED STATES of America,
Petitioner,
v.
Honorable Frank J. BATTISTI, Chief
Judge, United States District Court
for the Northern District of Ohio, Respondent.

No. 73-1177.

United States Court of Appeals,
Sixth Circuit
Oct. 25, 1973

Petition by the United States for writ of mandamus or prohibition to require the district court to vacate order which required recordation of all grand jury testimony and order which directed in certain criminal case that the Government produce names and addresses of all witnesses and all known records of prior criminal convictions of prospective witnesses. The Court of Appeals denied the application. On reconsideration, the Court of Appeals, Harry Phillips, Chief Judge, held that the recordation of grand jury testimony, although not required by the constitution or by statute, is the better practice. The Court further held that the order which required production of names and addresses of prospective witnesses and of known prior criminal records of prospective witnesses was an appealable order and that mandamus would not lie.

Order in accordance with opinion.

Apparently, the government was trying to protect some fairly disreputable stool pigeons and Judge Battisti wasn't having any of it.

Which is exactly what he was supposed to be doing. A really unusual case.

So how do you file petitions for Writs of Mandamus or Writs of Prohibition?

If you're not ready for "big game" yet (judges) and want to practice up on some smaller fry pick on a minor federal bureaucrat. You probably won't win in federal court but you'll insure that a copy of the lawsuit goes in his personnel dossier (or file)—meaning, when several people are considered for promotion, that all his superiors will figure he is incompetent and pass him over. I did this to a caseworker in Terre Haute and the results surpassed my wildest expectations. I ran three different prisoner lawsuits (filed by three different prisoners) in on him within a six week period and the prison administration fired him. Last I heard he had a paper route to feed himself.

Ironically, a lot of other prison personnel were happy to see him canned. His nickname was "the human slug".

To file such a petition you invoke jurisdiction under 28 USC 1361 and F.R. Civ. P. 81. Sometimes you can file it where you feel like under the provisions of 28 USC 1391. However, it will almost always be transferred to suit the bureaucrat. The rest of it is just like a standard lawsuit. Only the "relief requested" and "legal claims" are different.

At the end of this chapter is a sample mandamus petition. Watch the career of the female named at the head of the complaint—she'll probably wind up on the U.S. Supreme Court.

Why?

Because her legal acumen is worse than most. In one case I worked on, while she was still a District Court Judge in Detroit, she sentenced a man to 15 years in prison when the U.S. Code only allowed a 10 year maximum and THEN refused to alter the sentence. The very Court of Appeals she sits on now had to straighten her out.

As you can see from the sample documents beginning on the next page, she doesn't understand Title 28 and the Judiciary Act of 1789 any better than she did the sentencing provisions of Title 18:

ART. III—JUDICIAL DEPARTMENT

Sec. 2-Jurisdiction C1 1-Diversity of Citizenship

CONTROVERSIES BETWEEN CITIZENS
OF DIFFERENT STATES

The records of the Federal Convention are silent with regard to the reasons the Framers included in the judiciary article jurisdiction in the federal courts of controversies between citizens of different States, but since the Judiciary Act of 1789 "diversity jurisdiction" has been bestowed statutorily on the federal courts. The traditional explanation remains that offered by Chief Justice Marshall. "However true the fact may be, that the tribunals of the states will administer justice as impartially as those of the nation, to parties of every description, it is not less true that the Constitution itself either entertains apprehensions on this subject, or views with such indulgence the possible fears and apprehension of suitors, that it has established national tribunals for the decision of controversies between aliens and a citizen, or between citizens of different states."

SAMPLE DOCUMENT

In The
UNITED STATES SUPREME COURT

Michael H. Brown,
Petitioner

v. In Re Brown

Hon. Cornelia Kennedy
Hon. Nathaniel Jones
Hon. Harry Phillips,
Respondents

PETITION FOR WRIT OF MANDAMUS

I STATEMENT OF THE CASE

1. The cause arises out of the refusal of the above-named federal judges to rule on an issue raised on appeal No. 79-3195 in the Sixth Circuit, Appendixes A and B. The original complaint is given in Appendix C. The court's ruling is given in Appendix D.

II JURISDICTION

Jurisdiction is invoked under 28 USC 1651.

III PETITIONER

2. Petitioner is a pro se litigant attempting to litigate a civil action in federal court under 28 USC 1332, said action is Appendix C.

IV RESPONDENTS

3. Respondents are all federal judges on the Sixth Circuit Court of Appeals, Cincinnati, Ohio.

V FACTS

4. Respondents have all refused to rule - one way or the other - as to whether the lower federal court had jurisdiction of the case, Appendix C.

5. What the respondents did was issue a ruling for only some of the issues raised - those favorable to the defendants. 28 USC 1332 was ignored totally.

6. The trial court allowed the plaintiff to dismiss Richard Rose - a Kentucky resident and as such would have caused 28 USC 1332 to be non-applicable - and then arbitrarily dismissed plaintiff's complaint for "lack of subject matter jurisdiction".

7. This point, (6), was not ruled on in the Appeals Court either.

VI LEGAL CLAIMS

8. A judgment may be rendered withour an opinion, F.R. App. Pr. 36.

9. There is no legal provision for <u>any</u> court in the United States to rule on one issue favorable to one party and simply ignore the rights of the second party.

10. The respondents have conspired - arbitrarily and apparently maliciously - to deprive the petitioner of an absolute constitutional right; that of invoking "diversity jurisdiction" in a civil action guaranteed by the Judiciary Act of 1789, Article III, Section 2, U.S. Constitution, and later codified as 28 U.S.C. 1332.

11. The constitutional rights of the petitioner do not lie dependent upon the whim and caprice of members of the Sixth Circuit Court of Appeals.

12. The plaintiff has an absolute right to a COMPLETE ruling on his appeal, Appendix B.

13. Reasons the relief sought is not available in any other court:

A. The Sixth Circuit answers only to the Supreme Court. There is no other, higher court.

B. Justice delayed is justice denied. There is simply no need for this cause to wait until October, 1981 to be granted certiorari.

C. There is no need for the Supreme Court to grant (or deny) a question this simple (and obvious).

D. Certiorari is not a right of the petitioner's - his chances of obtaining review of his grievance are less than 1 in 100. In which case - relief on this petition denied, certiorari denied on review - it becomes patently obvious that the constitution (at least Article III, section 2) simply does not exist for the petitioner and others like him and is strictly dependent upon the whim and caprice of the federal judiciary.

RELIEF REQUESTED

1. That the respondents named - individually and severally - be commanded to answer the question: did the District Court in Lexington properly dismiss the original complaint, Appendix C, under the provisions of 28 USC 1332?

Yes?

Or No?

2. Given the apparent bad faith of the respondents the petitioner further requests that the Supreme Court order the lower court to furnish the petitioner with the laws and case cites necessary concerning their ruling (i.e., a total blank) in order to justify said ruling.

Respectfully Submitted,

Michael H. Brown

Michael H. Brown
101 Cherry Road
Berea, KY 40403

ANCILLARY MOTION

Petitioner requests this court grant him an extension of time to petition for certiorari; such extension to run sixty (60) days after the court's ruling on this petition for Writ of Mandamus.

Michael H. Brown

Michael H. Brown

SAMPLE DOCUMENT

CERTIFICATE OF SERVICE

This is to certify that I have on this ____ day of __________, ____ placed a true and exact copy of the foregoing in the U.S. Mails via certified mail addressed to:

Hon. Cornelia Kennedy
Sixth Circuit Court of Appeal
Cincinnati, Ohio

Hon. Nathaniel Jones
Sixth Circuit Court of Appeal
Cincinnati, Ohio

Hon. Harry Phillips
Sixth Circuit Court of Appeal
Cincinnati, Ohio

Hon. Edward Panzer
299 Broadway
New York, New York 10007

Hon. Lyle Robey
STOLL, KEENON, & PARK
1000 First Security Plaza
Lexington, KY 40507

Nolan Carter, Jr.
BOEHL, STOPHER, GRAVES & DEINDOERFER
710 First National Building
Lexington, KY 40507

Michael H. Brown
Michael H. Brown

SAMPLE DOCUMENT

No. 79-3195

MICHAEL H. BROWN)
)
Plaintiff-Appellant)
)
v.)
)
EDWARD S. PANZER, ARTHUR HANES, JR.)
MICHAEL YOUNG, PHYLLIS SKLOOT BAMBERGER,)
AND WILLIAM J. GALLAGHER)
)
Defendants-Appellees)

MOTION FOR COMPLETED RULING

* * * * * * * * * *

Comes the plaintiff in the above numbered cause, Michael H. Brown, pro se, and moves the court to complete their order, to writ:

Did the District Court have jurisdiction under 28 USC 1332?

Yes?

Or no?

It is patently obvious that the appellate court judges have simply sidestepped the issue in order to affirm the District Court's erroneous decision, in bald defiance of the intention of Congress in enacting 28 USC 1332.

Plaintiff-appellant cannot appeal an issue to the Supreme Court that has not been ruled on by the Appeals Court.

Respectfully Submitted,

Michael H. Brown
101 Cherry Road
Berea, Kentucky 40403

Appendix A

SAMPLE DOCUMENT

JOHN P. HEHMAN
CLERK

OFFICE OF THE CLERK
UNITED STATES COURT OF APPEALS
FOR THE SIXTH CIRCUIT
CINCINNATI, OHIO 45202

November 10, 1980

Mr. Michael H. Brown
101 Cherry Road
Berea, Kentucky 40403

Re: Case No. 79-3195
Michael H. Brown, Plaintiff-Appellant, vs.
Edward S. Panzer, et al, Defendants-Appellees.

Dear Mr. Brown:

This letter is in reply to your "Motion for Completed Ruling" recently received in this office. As its order of October 27, 1980, indicates, the Court was not of the opinion that the question you now raise concerning district court jurisdiction under 28 U.S.C. §1332 needed to be addressed in coming to its decision.

Please be advised that the October 27, 1980 order represents the final judgment of the Court in this appeal, review of which can now be sought in the Supreme Court if you are so inclined.

Very truly yours,

Leonard Green

Leonard Green
Case Manager

LG/rew

cc:

Mr. Gregory K. Jenkins
Boehl, Stopher, Graves
& Deindoerfer
710 First National Building
Lexington, Kentucky 40507

Appendix B

SAMPLE DOCUMENT

NO. 79-3195

UNITED STATES COURT OF APPEALS

FOR THE SIXTH CIRCUIT

FILED

OCT 2? 1980

JOHN P. HEHMAN, Clerk

MICHAEL H. BROWN,

Plaintiff-Appellant,

v.

EDWARD S. PANZER; ARTHUR HANES, JR.; MICHAEL YOUNG: PHYLLIS SKLOTT BAMBERGER; AND WILLIAM J. GALLAGHER,

Defendants-Appellees.

O R D E R

BEFORE: KENNEDY and JONES, Circuit Judges, and PHILLIPS, Senior Circuit Judge

Brown, appearing pro se, appeals the dismissal, by the Eastern District of Kentucky, of his complaint alleging attorney malpractice and breach of contract. He sought damages. The district court dismissed the complaint for failure to state a claim, improper venue, and lack of subject matter jurisdiction. We affirm.

I.

On September 6, 1974, Brown was indicted in the Southern District of New York on four counts for his involvement in placing an explosive device at the United Nations headquarters. He was acquitted on a conspiracy count. He was convicted for attempting to assault with a deadly weapon (count two), attempting to injure real and personal property (count three), and transporting an explosive device in interstate commerce (count four). He was sentenced to ten, five and ten year concurrent sentences, respectively. The Federal Defender Services

Appendix C

Unit of the Legal Aid Society of New York was assigned to represent Brown on appeal. On November 18, 1975, the Second Circuit affirmed Brown's conviction on counts three and four and vacated count two (knowingly attempting to injure real and personal property and occupied by an international organization) by an oral opinion from the bench. Brown was resentenced on count four to five years. All these events occurred in New York State.

On August 24, 1978, Brown filed a complaint in the Eastern District of Kentucky alleging that his trial and appellate counsel failed to adequately represent him. Brown contends that his attorney failed to raise during trial the fact that the FBI tampered with Brown's mail while he was in the Fayette County Jail. Brown's appellate pro se brief states that his attorney's action resulted in the loss of federal habeas corpus review, 28 USC §2255, by the Southern District of New York. He also alleged that the trial and appellate counsel failed to consult with Brown on strategy.

II.

Federal courts have jurisdiction when a case arises under the Constitution, laws or treaties of the United States within the meaning of 28 USC §1331. To determine if a federal question exists the face of a well pleaded complaint must be examined. Louisville & Nashville R.R. Co. v. Motley, 211 US 149 (1908). The claim therein must be founded on a federal right such that the right would be supported if the United States Constitution or laws are given one construction or effect and defeated if given another. Gully v. First National Bank, 299 U.S. 109 (1936). Applying these principles to this action, we conclude that the district court did not err in holding that Brown's complaint did not allege a federal question. There is no federal common law applicable to Brown's complaint alleging legal malpractice. Brown's allegations can be adjudicated only under state law.

In a case where subject matter jurisdiction is founded upon 28 USC §1331, the applicable venue statute is 28 USC §1391(b). Venue is proper in the jurisdiction where all the defendants reside or where the cause of action arose. Applying this statute to the facts of this case, venue was proper only in New York, the place where the cause of action arose. All of the defendants do not reside in Kentucky.

Accordingly, the judgment of the district court is AFFIRMED.

ENTERED BY ORDER OF THE COURT

John A Hehman
Clerk

SAMPLE DOCUMENT

IN THE

UNITED STATES DISTRICT COURT

FOR THE EASTERN DISTRICT OF KENTUCKY

MICHAEL H. BROWN Plaintiff v F. SALTEN EDWARD S. PANZER ARTHUR HANES, JR. MICHAEL YOUNG PHYLLIS SKLOOT BAMBERGER WILLIAM J. GALLAGHER RICHARD ROSE Defendants	)	Civil Action No.________ NEGLIGENCE & LEGAL MALPRACTICE

I. JURISDICTION

1. Jurisdiction of this court is invoked under the Constitution and laws of the United States as follows:

A. 28 USC 1331(a) in that the actions of the defendants herein constitute violation of the Constitution and laws of the United States and two (2) of the defendants are Federal employees.

B. 28 USC 2201 and 2202.

C. 28 USC 1332(a) (1) in that plaintiff Brown and defendant Rose are residents of Kentucky, defendant Hanes is a resident of Alabama, and defendants Salten, Panzer, Young, and Bamberger are residents of New York.

II. VENUE

2. Venue is proper under:

A. 28 USC 1391(e)(4) in that plaintiff Brown is a citizen and defendants Young and Bamberger are Federal employees.

III. PARTIES

Appendix D

(This document is a facsimile which was re-typed to improve legibility. For a reproduction of the original document, turn to page 187.)

SAMPLE DOCUMENT

3. Plaintiff Brown has a legal residence of 101 Cherry Rd., Berea, Kentucky 40403.

4. Defendant F. Salten is and was at all times mentioned herein the clerk, United States District Court, Southern District of New York, Foley Square, New York 10007.

5. Defendant Edward S. Panzer was, at the time of the actions complained of herein, the plaintiff's "advocate," one of two (2). His address was 299 Broadway, Suite 605, New York, New York 10007.

6. Defendant Arthur Hanes, Jr., 6718 Frank Nelson Building, Birmingham, Alabama, was, at the time of the actions complained of herein, the defendant's attorney, hired by his mother, for the trial of an indictment found September 6, 1974 in the Southern District of New York.

7. Defendant Michael Young was the public defender subsequently assigned to prosecute the plaintiff's appeal after the plaintiff's conviction.

8. Defendant Phyllis Skloot Bamberger is the head of the Public Defender's Office in Foley Square and as such is responsible for the orderly running of that office.

9. Defendant William J. Gallagher was listed as "Attorney for Defendant" on plaintiff's appeal brief submitted by Michael Young at Foley Square.

10. Defendant Richard Rose was the Public Defender in Lexington, Kentucky appointed to the plaintiff during the month of September, 1974 and as such was informed of the unlawful conduct of the FBI.

IV. FACTS

11. The plaintiff was arrested September 10, 1974 and transferred to New York on October 1, 1974.

12. During the time the plaintiff was incarcerated in the Fayette County jail, the FBI indulged in extensive tampering with plaintiff's incoming and outgoing correspondence.

13. Defendant Panzer was notified of the mail tampering issue via a carbon copy of a letter sent to the trial judge on October 9, 1974.

14. Defendant Panzer neither filed any motion objecting to such

conduct by the FBI nor informed the plaintiff that such actions constituted Fourth Amendment violations.

15. Defendant Panzer talked to the plaintiff only once before trial, informed him his fingerprints were all over the evidence (a lie), and attempted to coerce the plaintiff into an insanity defense.

16. Defendant Panzer refused to communicate with the plaintiff before trial, made no attempt to prepare any type of defense, and as a result the plaintiff's mother was forced to hire defendant Hanes. Defendant Hanes paid defendant Panzer a substantial sum to assist in the plaintiff's defense and defendant Panzer then "called in sick" the day of the trial and did nothing further for the defendant.

17. Defendant Hanes also refused to raise the Fourth Amendment issue, mail tampering, with the trial court either before, during, or after trial though he had knowledge of it.

18. Defendant Salten was negligent in the handling of plaintiff's case in that when she transferred the plaintiff's transcript of trial she "neglected" to enclose the plaintiff's pre-trial motion and correspondence.

19. Defendants Young and Bamberger were negligent in (1) their procurement of the plaintiff's <u>complete</u> trial and pre-trial proceedings and (2) in their willful failure to communicate with the plaintiff before they submitted an appeal brief on his case. Evidently, neither of them were aware of the plaintiff's pre-trial motions or deliberately bypassed them.

20. As a result of the defendants' combined negligence, the District Court of the Southern District of New York denied a 28 USC 2255 proceeding April 22, 1977 deeming the issue had been "deliberately bypassed" and "waived" and the Second Circuit Court of Appeals affirmed that decision on November 2, 1977.

21. Such "bypass" and waiver was solely the fault of the defendants as the plaintiff had no formal training in law, was not aware of 18 USC 1701 and 1702 until September of 1976 while the 2255 petition was being prepared and was unaware that such conduct constituted a Fourth Amendment" violation until it was pointed out by the U.S. Attorney in the response to that 2255 petition.

SAMPLE DOCUMENT

V. LEGAL CLAIMS

22. The four elements of negligence are present in the instant case:

A. A duty, or obligation, recognized by the law, requiring the actor to conform to a certain standard of conduct, for the protection of others against unreasonable risks.

B. A failure on their part to conform to the standard required.

C. A reasonable close causal connection between the conduct and the resulting injury.

D. Actual loss or damage resulting to the interests of another.

23. The four elements of legal malpractice are also present:

A. Contract for professional service.

B. Reliance by plaintiff.

C. Failure to exercise professional skill.

D. Damage caused by that failure.

24. The plaintiff, unable to litigate and/or vindicate a Constitutional right because of the negligent conduct of the defendants, in addition to the extra time he has spent in prison, must live in fear of being "violated" on parole until September 10, 1979 and spend the rest of his life deprived of his rights under the Second Amendment, the right to own firearms.

RELIEF REQUESTED

1. Compensatory damages in the amount of $50,000 from each defendant.

2. Punitive damages in the amount of $50,000 from each defendant.

3. Trial by jury on all issues triable by jury in accordance with the provision of Federal Rule of Civil Procedure 38(a) and (b).

4. Plaintiff's cost of this action.

5. Such other relief as this Court deems just, proper, and equitable.

NOTARY PUBLIC

RESPECTFULLY SUBMITTED,

____

MY COMMISSION EXPIRES:

____

MICHAEL H. BROWN
101 CHERRY ROAD
BEREA, KENTUCKY 40403

The reason I say that Cornelia Kennedy will make the Supreme Court behaving like this is that—once her antics become public—it gives all the male chauvinists in Congress an EXCELLENT excuse to keep further females off the nation's highest court. According to the Bible there shouldn't be any women in such position anyway:

"But I suffer not a woman to teach, nor to usurp authority over the man, but to be in silence." (I Timothy 2:12)

Ever consider that this may be one of our nation's primary problems—Congress thinks itself wiser than God?

Before we go any further there is another note of caution I want to interject here.

If a federal judge acts like he is even remotely sympathetic to your cause, WATCH YOURSELF. He is normally setting a trap for you.

This is partially what happened to me on the preceeding case. It was my fault, I knew better, I'd been through it before.

Cornelia Kennedy had scheduled the case for oral argument, Oct. 6, 1980 in the Sixth Circuit Court of Appeals. I argued my side of it, stressing the legislative history of 28 USC 1332 and pointing out that under the liberalized provision of that statute Congress allows me to sue someone in Saudi Arabia but the lower court wouldn't allow me to sue a bunch of attorneys in New York and Alabama.

None of the three appeals court judges so much as mentioned 28 USC 1332. Judge Jones kept asking me if this was a "Sixth Amendment" question (ineffective assistance of counsel) under 28 USC 1331. He seemed so sincere (a black Uncle Tom type) that I let my guard down and allowed myself to be led off into that line of questioning.

Judge for yourself what the results were (Petition for Writ of Mandamus, Appendix D).

Once you file a petition for Writ of Mandamus for anything other than nuisance or harrassment value your work has just started. The next step is to write your Congressman, the President, the newspaper, every member of the Senate Judiciary committee, and everyone else available pointing out the totally unlawful conduct of the judge. What will happen initially is that the Congressman's secretary will simply photocopy your letter, forward a copy to the offending party, photocopy the offending party's reply and mail it back to you with a note saying, "I hope this solves the problem."

It never does.

NOW what you have to do is write the Congressman AGAIN and explain why his reply wasn't satisfactory. It's not as much work as it seems.

For the initial letter to the Congressman and Senate Judiciary Committee, you simply go to the printer and have a hundred copies of the same letter printed up. Type in his name. Hand address the envelopes so they'll know a voter is involved.

The judge's secretary or U.S. Attorney (they are famous for attempting to curry favor with federal judges by doing unauthorized work for them) will send the EXACT same letter back to everyone who writes them.

Which makes your job even easier.

Simply pull the nonsense apart, rebut it, and go back to the printer.

It is highly unlikely that any immediate benefit to yourself will accrue. Congress, consisting of 96,000 lbs. of lawyers, is harder to move than a sperm whale on dry land, but other goodies come to the surface.

One is that you now have a wad of correspondence proving that at least one Congressman (yours) is totally ineffective when it comes to protecting the constitutional rights of his constituents (THAT is his primary function; not helping to pass tons of useless, needless laws). His opponent in the next election will love you for copies of such letters. What better way to unseat an incumbent than to prove—on TV and in the newspaper—that the incumbent is ineffective, unconcerned, operates like a bureaucrat, and is a weakling?

The other is that you may do your fellow taxpayers a tremendous service further on down the road. Any United States Senator who has gotten half a dozen detailed letters from one individual on one judge is going to remember it at a confirmation hearing to appoint someone to a position in the federal judiciary.

In a three-man race among judges the one who has had a hundred United States Senators receive complaints on him automatically comes in third.

Which means the lesser of three evils ascends to the bench.

The nation benefits.

7. The Appeal

This is your next step if a judge rules against you. In federal court it's not an "if", it's a "when". In many cases asking for a Writ of Mandamus merely gets you to this step. Sometimes merely filing a Notice of Appeal has strange consequences if the judge has already had to deal with you—and been ridiculed—a couple of times before.

In one case I wrote a habeas corpus petition for a diabetic in Terre Haute. The medical care at the prison was so bad that he had gone into insulin shock several times and simply been left on his back to come out of it by himself. During the time he was in Terre Haute, his eyesight started to go (blindness is common for diabetics given improper care), he could not control his bladder, and his feet developed ulcerous and open sores.

The habeas corpus alleged 8th Amendment, U.S. Constitution, violations as interpreted by the U.S. Supreme Court in *Estelle* v *Gamble* 50 L.Ed. 2d 251 and asked for his release. The case was docketed May 12, 1978.

The federal government simply has no authority to torture the sick.

At least, not in that fashion.

Judge James E. Noland airily dismissed the case on October 24, 1978. At this time I had been out of prison since January 4 of the same year. Noland knew—as did all the other federal judges in the Southern District of Indiana—that I considered their District Court as a mere administrative procedure that I had to go through to get to where the REAL courts (appeals) were. Since I had been out of sight for nine months he probably figured my "client" would just have to fend for himself. Apparently, the Bureau of Prisons was entitled to finish killing him.

As soon as I found out about it I filed a "Notice of Appeal", listing myself as "next friend".

The SAME DAY Judge Noland REVERSED HIMSELF and reopened the case. That is, to him the U.S. Constitution and federal law meant one thing before he knew he was going to be ridiculed in the Court of Appeals and the EXACT OPPOSITE the next day!

Judge Noland then scheduled an in-person hearing for my friend, March 9 of the next year.

Which, of course, gave the Bureau of Prisons long enough to get my diabetic out on a parole so that the judge could then dismiss the action as "moot"—which he did on May 17, 1979.

Still, my man was luckier than a lot of them. When I first got to Terre Haute in August, 1976 I sat down with two inmate medical assistants at chow in the mess hall and couldn't help overhearing their conversation.

A short while before they had been up in the prison hospital with an epileptic with emphysema, a black man. He was having an epileptic fit. The two inmates were ordered to hold his arms while a prison employee shot him full of thorazine to make him stop moving. The two inmates begged the guard to let him flop—the man was trying to keep his lungs clear of fluid.

The guard wouldn't listen.

The man died (or was killed).

His parents, working with a public-interest law firm in Chicago, filed a lawsuit against the prison. I believe it was dismissed as "frivolous".

Apparently niggers aren't worth much to the federal judiciary.

So how do you file an appeal?

First, you file a "notice of appeal", usually within 30 days of the District Court action giving you the shaft. It looks like this:

SAMPLE DOCUMENT

UNITED STATES DISTRICT COURT
SOUTHERN DISTRICT OF INDIANA
TERRE HAUTE DIVISION

HAROLD JAMES JENKS PLAINTIFF V KATY LOUDERMILK P. R. ROLLINS DEFENDANTS	))))))))))	FILE NUMBER TH 77-54-C NOTICE OF APPEAL

NOTICE IS HEREBY GIVEN THAT HAROLD JAMES JENKS, PETITIONER ABOVE NAMED, HEREBY APPEALS TO THE UNITED STATES COURT OF APPEALS FOR THE SEVENTH CIRCUIT FROM THE ENTRY OF JUDGEMENT BY THE DISTRICT COURT ENTERED IN THE ABOVE ACTION FEBRUARY 6, 1978.

RESPECTFULLY SUBMITTED,

HAROLD JAMES JENKS
REG. NO. 30636-117
P. O. BOX 33
TERRE HAUTE, IN 47808

...d by the Act of

Parole Officer

SUBSCRIBED AND SWORN TO BEFORE ME

THIS 21 DAY OF FEBRUARY, 1978.

UNITED STATES PAROLE OFFICER

SAMPLE DOCUMENT

CERTIFICATE OF SERVICE

I DO HEREBY CERTIFY THAT I HAVE ON THIS 21 DAY OF FEBRUARY, 1978 PLACED TWO (2) COPIES OF THE FOREGOING NOTICE OF APPEAL IN A POSTAGE PRE-PAID ENVELOPE, CERTIFIED MAIL, RETURN RECEIPT REQUESTED, ADDRESSED TO THE UNITED STATES DISTRICT COURT, SOUTHERN DISTRICT OF INDIANA, TERRE HAUTE DIVISION, TERRE HAUTE, INDIANA, 47803, AND CAUSED SAME TO BE PLACED IN THE UNITED STATES MAIL HERE AT THE UNITED STATES PENITENTIARY, TERRE HAUTE, INDIANA.

HAROLD JAMES JENKS
REG. NO 30636-117

SUBSCRIBED AND SWORN TO BEFORE ME
THIS 21 DAY OF FEBRUARY, 1978.

UNITED STATES PAROLE OFFICER

Authorized by the Act of
July 7, 1955 to Administer
Oaths (18 U.S.C. 4004)

Clifton E. Floyd
Parole Officer

As shown on the following page, if there are any mistakes or fees to be paid the court clerk will let you know what they are:

SAMPLE DOCUMENT

UNITED STATES DISTRICT COURT
OFFICE OF THE CLERK
SOUTHERN DISTRICT OF OHIO

JOHN D. LYTER
CLERK

DAYTON, OHIO 45402

April 5, 1977

Harold James Jenks
Reg. No. 30636-117
P.O. Box 33
Terre Haute, Indiana 47808

In re: Harold James Jenks
-v-
Katy Loudermilk, Et al
Civil No. C-3-77-71

Dear Mr. Jenks:

Enclosed is the Notice of Appeal regarding the above captioned matter.

Please be advised that there is a $5.00 filing fee and a $250.00 bond required in filing a Notice of Appeal

If you wish to file your Notice of Appeal in Forma Pauperis, please complete the enclosed Affidavit in support of Motion to proceed in Forma Pauperis, and return the affidavit and the Notice of Appeal to the office of the Clerk.

The Order transferring this case to the Southern District of Indiana was filed on March 28, 1977. Your appeal must be filed on or before April 28, 1977.

Very truly yours,

JOHN D. LYTER, CLERK

BY: C Makley
C. Makley, Deputy

cam
Encl.

In one case the nonsense we were appealing appears on the next three pages:

SAMPLE DOCUMENT

UNITED STATES DISTRICT COURT
SOUTHERN DISTRICT OF INDIANA
TERRE HAUTE DIVISION

MICHAEL H. BROWN and HAROLD JAMES JENKS, Plaintiffs,	)	
-vs-	)	NO. TH 78-117-C
KATHERINE LOUDERMILK, J.B. JOHNSON and J.W. JEAN, Defendants,	)	

E N T R Y

This cause came before the Court on the Complaint of Plaintiffs' and Defendants' Motion to Dismiss. The Court having examined said Complaint and Motion to Dismiss now finds that the said Motion to Dismiss should be sustained.

IT IS THEREFORE ORDERED that the Motion of the Defendants to dismiss Plaintiffs' Complaint is hereby SUSTAINED and this cause is hereby DISMISSED.

JAMES E. NOLAND, Judge
United States District Court

Dated: ______________

Memorandum

This Complaint was originally filed in the Eastern District of Kentucky where summons was ordered issued. Defendants, by Assistant United States Attorney, for said district, filed their Motion to Dismiss or in the Alternative to Transfer the cause to the Southern District of Indiana, which transfer was granted.

In the Complaint, Plaintiffs allege that it is for declaratory relief and damages because of Defendants' collective and deliberate

(This document is a facsimile which was re-typed to improve legibility. For a reproduction of the original document, turn to page 191.)

interference with Plaintiffs' rights of access to the Courts. Although Plaintiffs allege that Plaintiff Brown has a legal residence in Berea, Kentucky, they do not state the location of Plaintiff Jenks. Basically, Plaintiffs allege that Defendants conspired to deny Plaintiffs access to the Courts by refusing to file a "next friend" habeas corpus petition submitted by Brown on behalf of Jenks. Plaintiffs identify said petition for habeas corpus as TH 76-88-C. They further allege that due to Defendant Loudermilk's refusal, Plaintiff Brown did not receive a hearing on the habeas corpus petition from June 15 to November 23, 1976. Petitioners further allege that Defendant Loudermilk interferred with Brown's civil rights by unauthorized disclosure of information, that Loudermilk unlawfully caused the ruling on habeas corpus petition to be sent to wrong address and caused Brown to be threatened with disciplinary action by Defendant Jean if Brown wrote any more letters to Loudermilk. Plaintiffs pray for declaratory judgment, compensatory and punitive damages, costs and an order removing each defendant from government employment.

On July 14, 1978, the Assistant United States Attorney for the Southern District of Indiana filed an answer in admission and denial and that the Defendants as federal officers are immuned from liability for actions taken in good faith within the scope of their duties.

Plaintiffs' complaint fails to state a claim against Defendant Jean as the only reference to him is contained in paragraph 11, wherein Plaintiffs allege Jean and Johnson at the time "of the foregoing instance" were both Plaintiffs' caseworkers. The "foregoing instance" refers to alleged threat attributed to Johnson concerning further letters to Loudermilk. Plaintiffs' complaint fails to state a claim against Defendant Johnson as the allegation concerning the threat contributed to him is conclusory only and further does not rise to a constitutional level. The Plaintiffs' allegations concerning the Defendants conspiring to deny Plaintiffs access to the Courts is unsupported and conclusory only as to Jean and Johnson and contain no facts that any conspiracy existed or could be implied between them or with Loudermilk.

As to the alleged claim against Loudermilk, the record clearly shows that the alleged action or inaction by Loudermilk regarding the Petition for Habeas Corpus in TH 76-88-C, was within her capacity as Deputy Clerk of this Court. Indeed the exhibits attached to Petitioners' complaint evidence this fact. The other records of this Court show the legal reasons for the alleged delay complained of. While acting within her capacity as an officer of this Court, Loudermilk is immuned from suit. Even without immunity, there is not sufficient claim for which Loudermilk could be subject to any suit. The allegation that Loudermilk unlawfully caused the ruling on the habeas corpus petition to be sent to the wrong address fails to state a claim. Plaintiffs' claim that she caused Brown to be threatened by Jean with disciplinary action is completely unfounded and a conclusion and therefore fails to state a claim.

This same court clerk—Katherine Loudermilk—is sued for this type of behavior about once a year. In 1976 Jenks and me, in 1975 Harold Smith, in 1974 Paul Bijeol, etc. She's consistent.

In this case an appeal brief was somewhat hard to put together since what we were dealing with was a personality, no law, no case cites, no nothing.

So we simply attacked on that basis. Of course, the U.S. Attorney couldn't miss such an opportunity to toady to the judge, as you'll see on the following pages:

SAMPLE DOCUMENT

IN THE

UNITED STATES COURT OF APPEALS

FOR THE SEVENTH CIRCUIT

NO. 78-2507

MICHAEL H. BROWN and HAROLD JAMES JENKS, Plaintiffs-Appellants, v. KATHERINE LOUDERMILK, J. B. JOHNSON and J. W. JEAN, Defendants-Appellees.	Appeal from the United States District Court Southern District of Indiana Terre Haute Division (TH 78-117-C) Honorable James E. Noland District Judge

MOTION TO STRIKE BRIEF
OF APPELLANT BROWN

Defendants-appellees move this court to strike the Brief of Defendant-Appellant Michael H. Brown (styled "Brief for Appellants") on the ground that is contains nothing relevant to the resolution of the issues in this cause, and consists of nothing more than insulting references to the judiciary. *Pro se* litigants are not entitled to this latitude in pleading.

WHEREFORE, it is requested that appellant Brown's brief be stricken, and that this litigation be decided on the basis of the record and appellee's brief.

VIRGINIA DILL McCARTY
United States Attorney

By: Bradley L. Williams
Bradley L. Williams
Assistant United States Attorney

CERTIFICATE OF SERVICE

This is to certify that I have served a copy of the foregoing MOTION TO STRIKE BRIEF OF APPELLANT BROWN, upon the Plaintiffs-Appellants herein, by mailing a copy thereof to Michael H. Brown, 101 Cherry Road, Berea, Kentucky 40403 and Harold James Jenks, #30636-117, United States Penitentiary, Terre Haute, Indiana 47808, on this 23rd day of April, 1979.

Bradley L. Williams

Bradley L. Williams
Assistant United States Attorney

After the Notice of Appeal is filed you normally have so many days to prepare a brief, such number of days either outlined in the F.R. Civ. P. or ordered by the judge.

There isn't much to it—it's the claim, answer, and counterclaim business all over again. Only there's more paperwork involved.

The party appealing the case is the appellant.

The one appealed against is the appellee.

Since a judgement in the lower court can go either way a plaintiff or defendant can be either one.

A brief is simply a short booklet with the same type of heading as in the last motion. In place of "motion to strike" would be "briefs of plaintiffs-appellants" with your name and address on the lower right corner. Normally the color of the cover for appellants is blue, for appellees, red.

Inside the brief is broken down as follows:

1. Table of contents
2. Statement of the Case—that is, a brief summary of what happened originally.
3. Argument—an explanation of either why the lower court was wrong or why the other party was wrong to appeal it.
4. Conclusion—a one-paragraph summary of why the Appeals Court should rule in your favor.
5. Appendixes. In many cases this merely consists of the lower court complaint, answer, and court's ruling arranged in alphabetical order.

A "table of authorities" is normally given immediately following the table of contents.

Such authorities will be listed as:

Cases:	Page
Haines v. Kerner 404 U.S. 519 (1972)	5
Statutes:	
28 U.S.C. 2243	6,7
Rules:	
Fed. R. Civ. P. II	6

The cases are listed in alphabetical order. "Page 5" simply means that case is mentioned on page 5 of your brief.

A sample brief can normally be obtained by simply calling up a specialty printer for the legal profession—such as Westerfield-Bonte Co. in Louisville, Ky,—and asking for one. The last brief they printed for me they cleaned up a lot of my mistakes—such as putting my cases in alphabetical order.

Appeal briefs is an area the man acting as his own lawyer can shine in—the average lawyer never learned how to write one in law school (they normally don't teach it).

Again:

Appeal Brief

Appellee's Reply Brief

And correction of appellee's argument, if you feel like it.

Decision by a panel of judges.

Then—if possible—appeal to the NEXT higher court.

Sometimes you can't win no matter what you do. This is a case in point that you should be familiar with by now:

SAMPLE DOCUMENT

United States Court of Appeals

For the Seventh Circuit

Chicago, Illinois 60604

Submitted: July 31, 1979

... ORDER
... CATED
F... RULE 35

August 3, 1979.

Before

Hon. LUTHER M. SWYGERT, Circuit Judge

Hon. WALTER J. CUMMINGS, Circuit Judge

Hon. HARLINGTON WOOD, JR., Circuit Judge

MICHAEL H. BROWN and HAROLD JAMES JENKS, Plaintiffs-Appellants, No. 78-2507 vs. KATHERINE LOUDERMILK, J. B. JOHNSON, and J. W. JEAN, Defendants-Appellees.	Appeal from the United States District Court for the Southern District of Indiana, Terre Haute Division. No. TH 78-C-117 James E. Noland, Judge.

ORDER

Plaintiffs appeal from the district court's dismissal of their *pro se* civil rights action for failure to state a claim.[1/] Plaintiffs attempted to allege a conspiracy among the defendants to deny plaintiffs access to the courts. We affirm the district court's judgment.

1/ After preliminary examination of the briefs, the court notified the parties that it had tentatively concluded that oral argument would not be helpful to the court in this case. The notice provided that any party might file a "Statement as to Need for Oral Argument." *See* Rule 34(a), Fed. R. App. P. (effective Aug. 1, 1979); Circuit Rule 14(f). No such statement having been filed, the appeal has been submitted on the briefs and record.

No. 78-2507 Page 2

At the time they filed their complaint in this case Michael Brown and Harold Jenks were incarcerated at the federal prison in Terre Haute, Indiana. The complaint names as defendants: Katherine Loudermilk, deputy clerk of the United States District Court for the Southern District of Indiana, Terre Haute Division; J. B. Johnson, caseworker at the prison; and J. W. Jean, counselor at the prison. These defendants are alleged to have conspired to deny plaintiffs access to the district court in a number of lawsuits plaintiffs were litigating.

The complaint first alleges that "defendant Loudermilk jeopardized and interfered with the legal and civil rights of plaintiff Brown by unauthorized disclosure of information . . . ." Complaint, ¶ 4. The information referred to was a letter written by Brown to the district court requesting that the court forward habeas corpus forms to another inmate and indicating that Brown intended "to file a 'next friend' habeas corpus" for the other inmate. Loudermilk forwarded the letter to a Mr. Johnston "for [his] consideration." The complaint does not indicate who Mr. Johnston is[2/] or how his "consideration" of Brown's letter in any way interfered with Brown's access to the court. Nor is there any indication how Loudermilk's action in forwarding Brown's letter to Johnston violated Brown's right. The complaint does not allege that the requested habeas corpus forms were withheld or any other interference with Brown's access to the court. And if Brown is asserting some sort of privacy right, it is clear that he had no such right in the letter, which he made a public document when he filed it with the court. See Cox Broadcasting Corp. v. Cohn, 420 U.S. 469 (1975).

The complaint next asserts that Loudermilk conspired to deny Brown and Jenks access to the court by refusing to file a habeas corpus petition submitted by Brown on Jenks' behalf. Complaint, ¶ 5. The letter from the clerk's office attached to the complaint explains why the petition could not be filed and shows that the refusal to file it was justified.

2/ There is nothing in the complaint or the record identifying Mr. Johnston. If Brown intended to allege that Mr. Johnston was in fact defendant J. B. Johnson, the complaint fails to do so. As shown in the text, however, even if Johnston and Johnson are the same person, Brown has not alleged how the receipt and consideration of the letter violated any of his rights.

Plaintiffs' third allegation is that on July 27, 1976 Loudermilk failed to "record" the filing of a "Motion to Issue Show Cause Order" filed by Brown in a habeas corpus action he was litigating on his own behalf. Complaint, ¶ 6; see Brown v. Williams, No. 77-1228 (7th Cir. Feb. 26, 1979) (unpublished order; appeal from TH 76-88-C dismissed as moot). Brown does not allege that the motion failed to reach the court or how the alleged failure to record it otherwise interfered with his access to the court. Moreover, the record in that habeas corpus case shows that the district court did receive the motion and granted it on August 23, 1976.3/ In addition, Brown's July 27 motion is listed on the district court's docket sheet. Thus it is impossible to tell what Brown meant by alleging that Loudermilk "failed to record" his motion.

Brown's allegation that Loudermilk violated his rights by refusing to schedule a hearing on his habeas corpus petition, Complaint, ¶ 7, is frivolous. Only the court can schedule such a hearing.

Brown further alleges that "Loudermilk telephoned the Terre Haute pentitentiary and through her unlawful influence caused the ruling on [his] habeas corpus petition . . . and all other legal and personal mail belonging to [Brown] to be misrouted to a Community Treatment Center (Talbot House) in Ohio in an attempt to prevent plaintiff Brown from prosecuting an appeal" in TH 76-88-C. Complaint, ¶ 9 (emphasis added). This allegation fails to state a cause of action against Loudermilk for interfering with Brown's access to the courts for two reasons. First, Brown has failed to allege any facts to connect Loudermilk with the misrouting of his mail. The emphasized portion of the allegation above is Brown's only attempt to do so and is a legal conclusion, not a factual allegation. The records of the district court show that the order dismissing Brown's habeas corpus petition was sent to Brown at the prison and Brown has not alleged how a phone call from Loudermilk to the prison caused the order to end up in Ohio nor any facts constituting the alleged "unlawful influence."

3/ On May 31, 1979 this court granted the defendants' motion to take judicial notice of the court's records "to the extent that they are relevant." We note that the district court's order granting Brown's July 27, 1976 motion begins: "This cause comes before the court upon the motion of the petitioner, Michael H. Brown . . . ." The document immediately preceding that order in the district court's file in TH 76-88-C is Brown's July 27 motion.

No. 78-2507 Page 4

Second, even if Loudermilk did cause the decision to be sent to the wrong address, such conduct would not deny Brown access to the courts. Rule 77(d), Fed. R. Civ. P., makes it clear that the parties are responsible for keeping track of the status of their case and the need for filing a notice of appeal. Kramer v. Am. Postal Wkrs. Union, 556 F.2d 929 (9th Cir. 1977). "Notification by the clerk is merely for the convenience of litigants." Notes of Advisory Committee, Rule 77(d), 28 U.S.C.A. Since Brown was responsible for learning of the decision and filing his notice of appeal -- which he did, see Brown v. Williams, supra -- notice by the clerk, or the lack of it, could not affect his right of access to the courts.

Brown's final allegation is that after he wrote a letter to Loudermilk inquiring into the status of his various lawsuits, defendant Jean threatened him with "disciplinary action" if he wrote any more letters to Loudermilk. Complaint, ¶ 10. Once again, Brown has failed to allege how Jean's alleged threat interefered with his access to the courts or any other right. Brown has no constitutional right to direct his letters to defendant Loudermilk. He has not alleged that Jean's alleged threat intimidated him in any way or deterred him from vigorously pursuing any of his numerous lawsuits. And the records of this court show that he was not so deterred. Furthermore, Brown does not allege and the record does not show that the threatened disciplinary action would have been unjustified or would have been imposed without notice of the improper conduct charged and a hearing on such charges. In short, paragraph ten does not allege a violation of any of Brown's rights.

For the reasons stated above, none of the allegations in the complaint state a claim of denial of access to court or of any other constitutional right. Therefore, the judgment of the district court dismissing the action is affirmed.

What happened here?

As close as we could figure, the court clerk we were trying to drag into a jury trial was taking orders from "higher ups" — the judges themselves. That is, if she had been faced with losing a substantial amount of money because of her testimony on the witness stand under cross-examination she might have decided to rat on her co-conspirators — the judges.

Hence the prolonged cover-up.

The federal judiciary can be tamed—a subject which I shall cover in the last chapter.

It just can't be done by a couple of convicts from inside a federal prison.

8. Laying The Groundwork

In case you think it's strange to place this chapter after the ones on Appeal and Mandamus, there is a good, solid, logical reason for it.

It's called human nature.

Most people drive off into a how-to project, don't follow the directions, and then blame the author for their own mistakes.

What I HOPE I did in the previous chapters was give you an idea of what you're up against once the ball gets rolling.

A lot of such grief can be solved by one simple factor.

Careful preparation.

That is, if you prepare your case well enough, you may never have to litigate it. The really strong cases almost never wind up as "case cites" since the other side—the one that's going to lose takes one look and packs it in. This is especially true in cases that may become "case law". Better for the "bad guys" to roll over on one than to take a chance on losing in public and having every human filing exactly the same action.

How do you prepare a case?

First, research the law. Make sure you have your opponent by the legal throat. If it's questionable, forget it. It may blow up in your face. Besides, there's ALWAYS somebody to sue on an airtight case. People are constantly getting totally out of line.

Second, be able to PROVE your facts. Nowadays, about the only way to do that is to get your victim to commit himself to paper to where he can't retract anything later. Use a little imagination and it may not be as hard as you might think.

With federal employees it's a cinch. The most obvious way is the old "letter to the Congressman" trick—when you get back a self-serving reply from the bureaucrat that he wrote your Congressman THAT is what you attach to your civil action as Appendix A.

What we learned in Terre Haute was the "set-up".

It works like this:

Almost all federal agencies and large companies have some sort of grievance procedure you can go through. Most of the time what you get is the runaround. Which is to your advantage.

If a bureaucrat does what he's supposed to do—even if he does a lousy job—he's hard to hurt. Most of the time they don't, so not to worry.

What a systematic series of steps in a grievance procedure allows you to do is COLLECT EXHIBITS for your civil action.

In cases involving federal employees this can be devastating.

The following is a prime example of setting a bureaucrat up via an administrative form:

SAMPLE DOCUMENT

BP-9 June 21, 1976

This is a request directed towards Mr. Cox or whoever is responsible to answer the attached cop-out slip honestly, directly, and without equivocation or subterfuge.

STATEMENT OF FACTS

When I turned in this cop-out to Mr. Rollins we discussed it. He stated that he was not allowed to give me an answer in writing to the questions I asked on the cop-out.

I said fine, make that your answer.

He said that I did not understand and that they (?) had a meeting and that the questions I asked were some of the answers he was not allowed to give me in writing.

I said fine, make that his answer. He then said Mr. Cox was his boss and wanted to give me a pass to see Mr. Cox and if Mr. Cox told him to give him an answer in writing he would. I told him I was not going to see Mr. Cox and that he should see Mr. Cox and if Mr. Cox told him to give me an answer in writing then to do so and if not to answer the cop-out by saying Mr. Cox told him not to give me an answer in writing and that is what I would put on the BP-9.

Later that week I talked to Mr. Rollins and he said that after careful consideration he decided to give me an answer and I would have it the next day.

That was a week ago.

Refusal to answer a request under 5 USC 555(e) is a felony under 42 USC 1985 and is in addition a violation of 28 CFR p.200 appendix.

Once again I request an honest answer. If C&P personnel are incapable of an honest answer then please use that as your answer.

Footnote: This was not typed on an official government form since the form itself did not have enough room. "See attached" was typed on the form and the preceeding simply stapled on.

This was an Administrative Remedy form put out by the U.S. Bureau of Prisons, called a BP-9. The cop-out slip merely asked what criteria were used to classify prisoners as varying degrees of security risks. The administrators of the prison refused to answer it until they got several phone calls from the Terre Haute court clerk after we filed a petition—or should I say TRIED to file a petition—for a Writ of Mandamus to MAKE them answer the BP-9. This was the beginning of the *Loudermilk* case mentioned earlier in the book.

As you already know, we got buried on that one.

Over a year later we had "learned the ropes".

The federal prison system has an "administrative remedy" series of steps that go like this:

BP-9 The prison
BP-10 Appeal to Regional U.S. Bureau of Prisons
BP-11 Appeal to National U.S. Bureau of Prisons at D.C.

A lot of federal agencies have similar procedures. The idea is to minimize litigation. It never works that way since bureaucrats never try to fix anything, they just rubber-stamp denials or pass the buck. In many cases bureaucracies are infested by people who don't even know what their own rules are. The U.S. Parole Commission is famous for this. Quite often you can find rules in a collection of books titled C.F.R. (Code of Federal Regulations) and sold through the Superintendent of Documents, Washington D.C. U.S. Parole regulations, for example, are found in C.F.R. 28.

What we did on this one—and you can do the same thing in the same fashion with a lot of other government agencies, big corporations, and anyone or anything else that wants to get obstinate on paper—is to use the BP-9, 10, and 11 route ONLY to collect exhibits. Once we had received the usual collection of self-serving asininity from government employees we simply stapled them on the back as exhibits to a $250,000 civil action for deceit (as you may have guessed by now, one of my favorites).

What happened initially is that a caseworker had written a libelous progress report on my partner Jenks, Jenks filed a series of "remedies" because of it, and the warden promised him a new parole hearing that never materialized.

Since neither the warden or anyone else suspected we were "setting them up" they apparently felt no need to lie about what happened. By the time it got to the United States Attorney's office it was easier to give in than it would have been to litigate the issue (see next page).

SAMPLE DOCUMENT

OPTIONAL FORM NO. 10
JULY 1973 EDITION
GSA FPMR (41 CFR) 101-11.6

UNITED STATES GOVERNMENT

Memorandum

TO : Robert Vincent
Regional Commissioner

DATE: February 21, 1978

FROM : Rockne Chickinell
Regional Attorney

SUBJECT: JENKS, Harold James
30636-117

Assistant U.S. Attorney Brad Williams called on February 16 asking whether we would consider reopening Mr. Jenks' case to allow him to exhaust administrative remedies, or in the alternative, for a new hearing. In his litigation Jenks contends that the Bureau compiled an erroneous progress report before his June, 1977, hearing and that the panel relied upon this report to deny him parole. Subsequent to the denial the Bureau admitted its error and the warden promised him a new parole hearing. Mr. Jenks argues that he neglected his appellate rights from the June denial due to this representation. As the file reveals the Commission denied Mr. Jenks a new hearing and refused to hear his tardy appeal.

I believe we should give Mr. Jenks the benefit of the doubt here and acknowledge his claim that he forfeited his appellate rights based on the representations of institutional personnel. A new hearing appears to be the more proper remedy.

5010-112

This case would obviously never make the law books but it simply didn't matter to us. We had won.

I represented Jenks at his parole hearing a few weeks later. The parole examiners asked us directly about the lawsuit, seemed satisfied with our answers, and turned Jenks loose on parole shortly thereafter. Freedom, not money, was what we wanted in the first place.

To sum up: you can't over-prepare a case or have too much evidence on your side. If your groundwork is thorough enough you may not have to take a chance in front of a judge on a federal bench.

In a state case such preparation is almost always devastating to your opponent. I can almost guarantee you, your opponent's attorney will be the one that gives it up — and talks his client into surrendering — when he gets his with it.

Unless, of course, the client is merely to be "milked" for a sham defense.

9. Breaking The System

In the 1980 Presidential election the American people made it quite plain they weren't satisfied with their leaders. Could you imagine Tricky Dick or the Tooth Fairy being appointed for life?

Horrible thought, isn't it?

Yet that is exactly what has happened to the federal judiciary—and if you don't think they are our "leaders", talk to someone who is being victimized by forced bussing or some other judicial nonsense.

Nor is judicial misbehavior a new phenomenon. Andrew Jackson had repeated run-ins with the federal judges during his Presidency. Then, as now, they were more concerned with their own nonsense than they were in even-handedly applying the laws and the Constitution. This judicial arrogance has gone on unchecked for so long that the U.S. Constitution—as applied by the federal courts—simply no longer exists as a valid legal document. The words are there on the paper, but that's about all.

So how do we stop this rule by 10-cent tyrants that no-one elected in the first place?

The obvious solution is a Constitutional Amendment to limit federal judges to a specified number of years, just like the State Courts here in Kentucky. Unfortunately, convincing all of Congress that such a move is necessary would require so much money, manpower, and time that it would be self-defeating.

There are quicker, simpler ways.

As I hope I have made clear in this book there is only one way to deal with "public servants" that seems to work consistently: ask for what you want and if you don't get it give that particular "public servant" such a hard time that he will understand it would have been easier to do what you wanted and were entitled to in the first place. The old carrot and stick approach—only without the carrot. He got that when he cashed his paycheck, courtesy of the taxpayer.

Dealing with an entire corrupt system is somewhat more difficult than training an obnoxious bureaucrat or two. However, it's not impossible.

Let's take a couple of examples.

The first is trial by jury. In the federal courts the decision must be unanimous—all twelve—to send a man to prison. The longest prison terms are given to bank robbers—up to 25 years—even when no-one gets hurt and all the money is recovered.

Why?

In a copy of the Congressional Record I read during the Panama Canal give-away one Congressman inserted in the "Extensions of Remarks" section the real reason for that giveaway. Midland Marine, one of our nation's largest banks, had loaned Omar Torrijos so much money he couldn't afford to pay the interest, let alone any of the principal, back. Solution: give Torrijos the Panama Canal and let him double the rates in order to repay Midland Marine. "Our" Senate ratified that particular bank-engineered treaty.

The grain embargo was put on Russia because of their invasion of Afghanistan right?

Wrong.

According to another copy of the Congressional Record the Soviet Union has been bankrupt since August, 1976. They haven't even been able to pay the interest on their loans—to Chase Manhatten. The wheat was shut off simply because they couldn't pay for it.

In a "letter to the editor" series a few years ago William Steckler—chief federal judge for the Southern District of Indiana—complained bitterly about several bank robbery trials in which the jury found the suspects "not guilty".

Typical "impartial" federal judge.

Finally, one of the defense attorneys wrote in and told the rest of the story: the juries had become so disgusted with the government's paid informers and perjured testimony that they simply turned the obviously guilty parties loose.

Makes it pretty clear we're all ruled—one way or another—by the banks, doesn't it? Including the federal judiciary.

Meaning a federal judge who can't manipulate trials to send bank robbers to prison—consistently—isn't going to be on the bench long.

Federal juries are selected from the voter registration rolls. The odds of you being selected to sit on a bank robbery trial are pretty slim. There is another way.

Let's say you're in a town where forced bussing has been ordered by one of the cretins of the bench and your child is affected.

The first thing you do is file a Petition for Declaratory and Injunctive Relief with the federal court asking that your child be declared exempt from the bussing ruling on religious grounds. Forced mixing of races is a violation of the 19th Chapter of Leviticus in the Bible. If you're strictly a "New Testament Christian", pagan, or whatever then pack your kid on the bus and forget it. It's unlikely anything else will work.

Once your petition is filed one of two things will happen.

One is that the judge will sit on it.

The other is that he will rule against you.

If he sits on it, mandamus him. He'll still rule against you but at least you now have the ammunition required for the next step.

Which is not necessarily an appeal.

What you just did was ask the judge to declare whether his opinion or the First Amendment—freedom of religion—reigns supreme. In 99% of the cases the First Amendment gets thrown out the window.

Your next step is to find out how many other people agree with your viewpoint. In an area where forced bussing is mandatory there should be hundreds. Prepare a petition to your Congressman, not asking, but demanding:

We, the undersigned, demand that federal judge ________ ________ be removed from his position via impeachment before the next election. Should you fail to accomplish this, we the undersigned, will vote as a bloc to remove you in the next election and replace you with someone more attuned to the constitutional rights of his constituents.

____________________ ____________

Name (Signature) Address
etc.

Only Congress can impeach a federal judge. "Taming" a federal judge won't work simply because once the pressure is off they will revert to type. Removal, like cancer, is the only answer.

It doesn't take that many people to make a difference, either. Out of 180,000 registered voters in the Lexington, KY area only 11,000 showed up to vote in the 1978 Congressional election. Assuming a 51% - 41% Reagan-Carter style massacre 5610 people would have voted for the winner and 4510 for the loser. 552 people voting as a bloc could have tipped the election either way.

You don't think your Congressman will be able to get a federal judge impeached? Maybe not. But when you throw him out on his ear in the next election I can guarantee you that your NEXT Congressman will. You just have to make believers out of them.

The system can be broken.

You simply have to know where the machinery is and how it works before you can throw a monkey wrench in it. I hope I have provided that knowledge.

Appendix A

Original Document Reproductions

SAMPLE DOCUMENT

IN THE
UNITED STATES DISTRICT COURT
FOR THE SOUTHERN DISTRICT OF OHIO

HAROLD JAMES JENKS, Plaintiff	)	
v	)	Civil Action No. TH-77-54-C
	)	COMPLAINT
KATY LOUDERMILK P.R. ROLLINS, Defendants	)	

JURISDICTION

1. This action containing complaints for declaratory relief and for damages, is brought against the defendants to secure due process of law, equal protection and other rights, privileges and immunities guaranteed to complainant by the Constitution and laws of these United States.

2. Jurisdiction is invoked under the United States Code as follows:

A. 28 U.S.C. § 1331 in that the matter in controversy exceeds the sum of $10,000, exclusive of interest and cost, and arises under the Constitution and laws of the United States.

B. 28 U.S.C. § 1332(a)(1) in that the action arises between citizens of different States.

C. 28 U.S.C. § 1343

(1) To recover damages for injury to his person or property, or because of the deprivation of any right or privilege of a citizen of the United States, by any act done in furtherance of any conspiracy mentioned in section 1985 of Title 42;

(2) To recover damages from any person who fails to prevent or to aid in preventing any wrongs mentioned in section 1985 of Title 42 which he had knowledge were about to occur and power to prevent;

(3) To recover damages or to secure equitable or other relief under any Acto of Congress providing for the protection of civil rights, including the right to vote.

D. 28 U.S.C. § 2201 and 2202.

E. 42 U.S.C. § 1981.

F. 42 U.S.C. § 1985 and 1986.

G. All of the above statutes but not limited thereto.

VENUE

3. Venue for this action is proper under 28 U.S.C. § 1391(e)(4) in that the plaintiff has a residence of 717 Old Main Street, Miamisburg Ohio 45342 and 1037 Primrose Drive, West Carrollton, Ohio.

In determining domicile at common law, a change from one domicile to another requires proof. Together with physical removal of a person, there must be an accompanying intent to change domicile. Otherwise, the body will have moved, but the domicile will have remained where it was next in time prior thereto.

Ballas v Symm 351 F. Supp. 876, 886

There was no voluntary intent to change domicile by the plaintiff as he is a Federal prisoner:

Venue of action by federal prisoner was proper in district wherein petitioner was domiciled before his incarceration.

United States ex rel Harrison v Pace
357 F. Supp. 354

In action by federal prisoner against parole board seeking mandamus, venue was present under 28 U.S.C. § 1391(e) in district of prisoner's residence, even though prisoner was then incarcerated in different district.

Stone v United States Board of Parole
360 F. Supp. 22

Both defendants are Federal employees and the emphasis on venue under 28 U.S.C. § 1391(e)(4) should be readily self-evident upon a complete reading of the complaint.

SAMPLE DOCUMENT

PLAINTIFF

4. Plaintiff HAROLD JAMES JENKS is and was at all times mentioned herein a prisoner in custody of the United States Bureau of Prisons. He is currently confined in the United States Penitentiary, Terre Haute, Indiana.

DEFENDANTS

5. Katy Loudermilk is the Clerk of the Court for the Terre Haute Division of the United States District Court for the Southern District of Indiana.

6. P.R. Rollins was the caseworker assigned to the plaintiff during the time the incidents enumerated took place. He is currently employed in the Drug Abuse Program at Terre Haute penitentiary.

FACTS

7. In June 1976 the plaintiff's attorney, Mr. F. Dane Delcontive, mailed via certified mail two (2) petitions to the United States District Court from Dayton, Ohio. At the same time a check was mailed in the amount of $30.00 (thirty dollars) to insure prompt service on both petitions.

8. A few days after the petitions were mailed from Dayton the plaintiff walked into defendant ROLLINS office and the defendant was holding a telephone conversation. He (Rollins) did not notice the plaintiff standing in front of him. Defendant ROLLINS was writing something on a paper on his desk and talking to defendant LOUDERMILK on the telephone. The two defendants were discussing the mandamus petition the plaintiff had filed.

Defendant ROLLINS then looked up and saw the plaintiff standing in front of him. He turned white as if all the blood had drained from his face.

The plaintiff then inquired if defendant ROLLINS was talking to defendant LOUDERMILK about his case. Defendant ROLLINS sputtered and stammered and finally informed the plaintiff that defendant LOUDERMILK had called him and wanted to talk to the plaintiff. The plaintiff told defendant ROLLINS he was not allowed to discuss the plaintiff's petitions with the court clerk.

Defendant ROLLINS then hung up the telephone and refused to talk to the plaintiff.

One of the items overheard by the plaintiff said by defendant ROLLINS was, "Give me some time".

9. The mandamus petition filed in Terre Haute was to force the defendant ROLLINS to answer an Administrative Remedy Form (BP-9) that was out of time and the plaintiff had, before the mandamus action was filed, been informed by defendant ROLLINS that the BP-9 would not be answered.

10. Several days later, after the telephone call mentioned in (8), the plaintiff was summoned to the counselor's office and handed the BP-9 in litigation (the object of the mandamus) with an answer on it. The plaintiff asked his counselor, Mr. Barnett, why the BP-9 was finally answered several days out of time. Mr. Barnett informed the plaintiff that he did not know since he (Mr. Barnett) was also informed that the plaintiff would not receive an answer to his BP-9. The plaintiff then informed Mr. Barnett of the telephone call between defendants ROLLINS and LOUDERMILK. Mr. Barnett merely shrugged his shoulders and refused to comment further.

11. Several days later the plaintiff inquired of his attorney what the docket numbers on the two petitions were. He did not know and was under the impression the docket numbers and receipt for filing fee had been forwarded to the plaintiff from the District Court in Terre Haute. At this time the plaintiff's attorney was unaware of the telephone call between defendants ROLLINS and LOUDERMILK.

12. The next time the plaintiff talked to his attorney he was informed that the attorney had called the court and talked to Mrs. Loudermilk, was given the run-around, the petitions had not been filed, there were no docket numbers, his $30.00 check was returned, and she kept the petitions.

13. A week later the plaintiff again walked into defendant ROLLINS' office and again he was talking to defendant LOUDERMILK on the telephone. Defendant ROLLINS then handed the telephone to the plaintiff. Defendant LOUDERMILK then informed the plaintiff that she had just called to "explain to you what you have to do to get a docket number."

14. The plaintiff's girlfriend and her room-mate telephoned defendant LOUDERMILK, got nasty about it, and in November 1976, five months after the plaintiff tried to file his petitions, he received a docket number. One of the petitions had to be withdrawn since it was a FREEDOM OF INFORMATION ACT action that became mooted by the actions of defendant LOUDERMILK.

15. It took the plaintiff's attorney, Mrs. Sandy Egelston, Mrs. Carolyn Sue Hall, and the plaintiff through their combined efforts from July 1976 until November 1976 to get defendant LOUDERMILK to file one (1) petition.

LEGAL CLAIMS

16. The plaintiff, an American citizen, has an unqualified Constitutional right to access to the courts. The actions of the defendants not only precluded the plaintiff's lawful access to the Courts and denied him due process of law but were in addition felonies under Title 18, United States Code:

18 U.S.C. § 2 Whoever commits an offense against the United States or aids, abets, counsels, commands, induces or procures its commission, is punishable as a principal.

18 U.S.C. § 4 Misprision of a felony.

18 U.S.C. § 241 Conspiracy against rights of citizens.

18 U.S.C. § 371 Conspiracy to commit offense or to defraud United States.

18 U.S.C. § 401(2) Misbehavior of court officers in their official transactions.

18 U.S.C. § 1001 Lying and covering up.

18 U.S.C. § 1505 Obstruction of justice .

18 U.S.C. § 1905 Disclosure of confidential information.

And as of Sept. 28, 1976 no court clerk may refuse a petition. Public Law 94 - 426.

RELIEF REQUESTED

1. A declaratory judgement that the defendant's acts, policies, and practices described herein violate plaintiff's rights under the United States Constitution.

2. Compensatory damages in the amount of $50,000 from each defendant.

3. Punitive damages in the amount of $50,000 from each defendant.

4. Jury trial on all issues triable by jury.

5. Plaintiff's cost of this suit.

SAMPLE DOCUMENT

6. An Order removing both defendants LOUDERMILK and HOLLINS from Government employment consanant with 18 U.S.C. § 1905 which provides in part: "...and shall be removed from office or employment."

7. Such other relief as this Court deems just, proper, and equitable.

Respectfully Submitted,

HAROLD JAMES JENKS
Reg. No. 30636 - 117
P.O. Box 33
Terre Haute, Indiana 47808

Subscribed and Sworn to
before me this 24 day
of February, 1977.

UNITED STATES PAROLE OFFICER

Authorized by the Act of July 7, 1955
to administer oaths (18 U.S.C. 4004)

SAMPLE DOCUMENT

IN THE
UNITED STATES DISTRICT COURT
FOR THE SOUTHERN DISTRICT OF INDIANA
TERRE HAUTE DIVISION

HAROLD JAMES JENKS, MICHAEL H. BROWN, Plaintiffs v KATY LOUDERMILK, P.R. ROLLINS, J.B. JOHNSON, J.W. JEAN, Defendants	))))))))))))	Civil Action No. TH-77-54-C

AMENDMENT TO COMPLAINT

Come the plaintiffs in the above numbered cause, HAROLD JAMES JENKS and MICHAEL H. BROWN, and amend and supplement this complaint in accordance with Federal Rules of Civil Procedure 15(a)(c), 19(a)(1) - (2) and 20(a).

1. MICHAEL H. BROWN Reg. No. 81856, incarcerated at Terre Haute Prison, Terre Haute, Indiana 47808 is added as a plaintiff for any and several of the following reasons:

A. On March 23, 1976 defendant LOUDERMILK jeopardized and interfered with the legal and civil rights of plaintiff BROWN by unauthorized disclosure of information and other illegal acts enumerated in the original complaint (Appendix A) and in addition caused the plaintiff great mental distress.

SAMPLE DOCUMENT

B. On July 27, 1976 defendant LOUDERMILK failed to record a MOTION TO ISSUE SHOW CAUSE ORDER submitted by plaintiff BROWN in violation of the Federal statutes mentioned in the original complaint. The plaintiff has a copy in his possession of said MOTION stamped "filed" by the U.S. District Court, Terre Haute, and said motion does not appear on the docket sheet prepared by defendant LOUDERMILK.

C. Defendant LOUDERMILK refused to schedule plaintiff BROWN's habeas corpus petition, TH-76-88-C, in accordance with 28 U.S.C. § 2243 and Federal Rule of Civil Procedure 81(a)(2), causing plaintiff BROWN to take from June 15 to November 23, 1976 to get a hearing on his petition.

D. From information and belief defendant LOUDERMILK telephoned the Terre Haute prison and through her unlawful influence caused the ruling on said habeas corpus petition issued by the Court and all other legal and personal mail belonging to the plaintiff to be mis-routed to a Community Treatment Center (Talbott House) in Ohio in order to prevent plaintiff BROWN from prosecuting an appeal on said habeas corpus petition --- a situation remedied only by the due diligence of plaintiff BROWN.

E. On Dec. 8, 1976 plaintiff BROWN wrote defendant LOUDERMILK as to the status of his court proceedings. In consequence plaintiff BROWN was summoned to the counselor's office at 3:05 p.m. December 14, 1976 and before leaving at 3:40 p.m. that date threatened with "disciplinary action" by hereinafter named defendant J.W. JEAN if he (BROWN) wrote any more letters to defendant LOUDERMILK.

3. For the reasons given in 2(E) J.W. JEAN is added as a defendant.

4. For the following reasons J.B. JOHNSON is added as a defendant:

SAMPLE DOCUMENT

A. In August or early September 1976 plaintiff JENKS walked into defendant JOHNSON's office and found said defendant on the telephone conversing with defendant LOUDERMILK. Defendant JOHNSON immediately handed plaintiff JENKS the telephone. Plaintiff JENKS then inquired of defendant LOUDERMILK the reason(s) he had not received a reply to his correspondence requesting a docket number. Defendant LOUDERMILK replied that she had sent the plaintiff JENKS "several letters" detailing the problem. Plaintiff JENKS NEVER received any such letters nor were any to be found in his central file.

B. Judging from the foregoing it appears that J.B. JOHNSON and J.W. JEAN had joined in as willing co-conspirators.

Wherefore, the plaintiffs request this Court permit the foregoing amendment and supplementation to the original complaint and in addition:

1. That the Court order the defendants to retain their own personal counsel since the acts described in this complaint are not part of their jobs and

2. This Court prohibit the defendants, their employees, or associates from initiating retaliatory action against the plaintiffs for the filing of this action; such actions (usually) taking the form of "administrative" transfers, job changes, or other subtle forms of harrassment.

Subscribed and Sworn to
before me this 6 day
of May, 1977.

UNITED STATES PAROLE OFFICER

UNITED STATES PAROLE OFFICER

[illegible]

Respectfully Submitted,

Harold James Jenks
HAROLD JAMES JENKS
Reg. No. 30636 - 117

Michael H. Brown
MICHAEL H. BROWN
Reg. No. 81856 - 158

P.O. Box 33
Terre Haute, Indiana
47808

SAMPLE DOCUMENT

M.H. Brown
Reg. No. 81856
P.O. Box 33
Terre Haute, Indiana
March 9, 1976

RECEIVED
MAR 11 1976
U. S. CLERK'S OFFICE
TERRE HAUTE, INDIANA

138 (G)

Dear Sir:

Would you please send Harold Smith 30912-138 P.O. Box 33 Terre Haute, Indiana the necessary Habeas Corpus forms pursuant to Local Rule 25?

He is in "administrative segregation" for "convenience of the administration" reasons and I intend to file a "next friend" Habeas Corpus for him.

Thank You,

Michael H. Brown

3/23/76

Dear Mr. Johnston:

Pursuant to telephone conversation this date with a member of your staff, I am returning herewith the letter received in th office for your consideration.
Thank you very much.

Katherine [signature]
Deputy Clerk

88

SAMPLE DOCUMENT

Harold James Jenks
Reg. No. 30636-117
P.O. BOX 33
Terre Haute, Indiana
47808

Mr. Neil Smiley,

Just a note to let you know how things are going with me since I had my talk with you and also to ask you a question or two.

First of all I should let you know I am now paying the price for going to you for help.

When I left you a few weeks ago I went to see my team. You will find how I fared in the appendixes attached to this letter. Since that time I have talked to Mr. Wally Buer in the hallway of the C&P and tried to find out why such strong statements were made against me. Mr. Buer would not talk to me except to saw that he knew what I was trying to do and that I was not going to get away with it.

There are only two things he can be talking about. The first one is my legal work which they have been aware of for the past 14 mo., or two, the fact that I went to the F.B.I. for help.

My caseworker Mr. J.B. Johnson has never at any time in all the meetings I have had with him mentioned any of the things my team has used against me in the context they were used.

The questions I must ask you are (1) did you have a conversation with the staff, " inparticular Mr. Wally Buer " earlier on the day you talked to me. (2) Have you had a talk with any of the staff about me since then? I have seen you in the hall corrider 6 times so far and remender seeing you before I knew who you were. You must come up here a lot?

I am sorry to take up your time but I would like you to read my progress Report. The first 3 pages were done by my caseworker before I talked to you.

Page 2

Page 4 was done by my casemanagement team after I talked to you. The team is headed by Mr. Wally Buer.

The other letter is what I wrote to the Parole Board. I think the two are self explanatory. I go in front of the Parole Board the second week in June for my 1/3 hearing. What do you think my chances are NOW?

I would also like to know the name and address of the District Attorney you are talking to.

MORE GOOD NEWS: The original writ that Mrs. Loudermilk refused to docket in June 1976, and the subsequent phone calls to Mr. Hollins allowed them to answer the B.P.9 they refused to answer, and were out of time on before she finally gave me a docket number in December 1976.

I have just received a denial from Judge Dillon on my custody writ. The reason for denial was that I have not exhausted my administrative remedies. Mrs. Loudermilk's interference was directly responseable for this ruling. So far it has cost me a year's delay and looking forward to another year delay in the Appeals Court, along with all the money, effort, and time involved.

Request Responses As Soon As Possible.

Thank You,

cc: Mr. Hargraves

UNITED STATES COURT OF APPEALS
FOR THE SEVENTH CIRCUIT

HAROLD JAMES JENKS,)
MICHAEL H. BROWN,)
Plaintiffs)
)
v) Civil Action No.
) PETITION FOR WRIT OF PROHIBITION
)
CALE J. HOLDER,)
Defendants)

JURISDICTION

Jurisdiction of this court is invoked under 28 USC 1651.

PARTIES

The plaintiffs are federal prisoners incarcerated at Terre Haute federal prison, Terre Haute, Indiana.

The defendant is a federal judge in charge of the Terre Haute division of the Southern District of Indiana.

FACTS

1. The plaintiffs are scheduled for trial on December 22, 1977 9 a.m. at the Terre Haute courthouse by order of the defendant.

2. The defendant, it appears, has scheduled all Terre Haute prisoner complaints, including jury trials, for December 22, as he has done for a number of years.

3. The complaint scheduled for trial is one against the defendant's court clerk, Katy Loudermilk, docket number TH 77-54-C.

4. Based on (3), the defendants filed an affadavit of bias and prejudice against Judge Holder accroding to the provisions of 28 USC 144.

5. Based on past experience (see e.g. Brown v Williams 77-1228) the plaintiffs have no reason to believe that Judge Holder can conduct himself lawfully regarding the rights of prisoners: any judge who can schedule several "jury trials" with himself as presiding judge is in no way qualified to arbitrate fairly between the parties.

LEGAL CLAIMS

6. The three elements necessary for prohibition are present in the instant case:

A. That the person it is directed against is about to exercise judicial power.

B. That the exercise of such power by said person is unauthorised by law.

C. That it will result in injury for which there is no other adequate remedy.

7. The minute Judge Holder received the affadavit of bias and predjudice he lost jurisdiction over TH 77-54-C.

8. It is patently illegal for a judge to orchestrate several trials on the same day and at the same time; a courtroom is not a TV set where the viewer can change channels if he gets bored.

Subscribed and sworn to before me this 12 day of December, 1977.

UNITED STATES PAROLE OFFICER

UNITED STATES PAROLE OFFICER

Authorized by the Act of July 7, 1955 to administer oaths (18 U.S.C. 4004).

Respectfully Submitted,

Harold James Jenks
Reg No 30636 - 117

Michael H. Brown
Reg No 81856 - 158

P.O. Box 33
Terre Haute, Indiana 47808

CERTIFICATE OF SERVICE

This is to certify that I have on this 12 day of December, 1977 placed a true and exact copy of the foregoing in the U.S. Mails addressed to Hon Cale J Holder, U.S. District Court, Southern District of Indiana, Terre Haute Division, Terre Haute, Indiana 47808.

Harold James Jenks

SAMPLE DOCUMENT

IN THE

UNITED STATES DISTRICT COURT

FOR THE EASTERN DISTRICT OF KENTUCKY

MICHAEL H. BROWN Plaintiff v F. SALTEN EDWARD S. PANZER ARTHUR HANES, JR. MICHAEL YOUNG PHYLLIS SKLOOT BAMBERGER WILLIAM J. GALLAGHER RICHARD ROSE Defendants	)	Civil Action No.__________ NEGLIGENCE & LEGAL MALPRACTICE

I. JURISDICTION

1. Jurisdiction of this court is invoked under the Constitution and laws of the United States as follows:

A. 28 USC 1331(a) in that the actions of the defendants herein constitute violation of the Constitution and laws of the United States and two (2) of the defendants are Federal employees.

B. 28 USC 2201 and 2202.

C. goes here

II. VENUE

2. Venue is proper under:

~~A.~~ 28 USC 1332(a)(1) in that plaintiff Brown and defendant Rose are residents of Kentucky, defendant Hanes is a resident of Alabama, and defendants Salten, Panzer, Young, and Bamberger are residents of New York, ~~and the first-to-file principle should prevail.~~

B. 28 USC 1391(e)(4) in that plaintiff Brown is a citizen and defendants Young and Bamberger are Federal employees.

III. PARTIES

Appendix D

SAMPLE DOCUMENT

5. Plaintiff Brown has a legal residence of 101 Cherry Rd., Berea, Kentucky 40403.

6. Defendant F. Salten is and was at all times mentioned herein the clerk, United States District Court, Southern District of New York, Foley Square, New York 10007.

7. Defendant Edward S. Panzer was, at the time of the actions complained of herein, the plaintiffs "advocate", one of two (2). His address was 299 Broadway, Suite 605, New York, New York 10007.

8. Defendant Arthur Hanes, Jr., 6718 Frank Nelson Building, Birmingham, Alabama, was, at the time of the actions complained of herein, the defendants' attorney, hired by his mother, for the trial of an indictment found September 6, 1974 in the Southern District of New York.

9. Defendant Michael Young was the public defender subsequently assigned to prosecute the plaintiff's appeal after the plaintiff's conviction.

10. Defendant Phyllis Skloot Bamberger is the head of the Public Defenders Office in Foley Square and as such is responsible for the orderly running of that office.

11. Defendant William J. Gallagher was listed as "Attorney for Defendant" on plaintiff's appeal brief submitted by Michael Young at Foley Square.

12. Defendant Richard Rose was the Public Defender in Lexington, Kentucky appointed to the plaintiff during the month of September, 1974 and as such was informed of the unlawful conduct of the FBI.

IV. FACTS

13. The plaintiff was arrested September 10, 1974 and transferred to New York on October 1, 1974.

14. During the time the plaintiff was incarcerated in the Fayette County Jail, the FBI indulged in extensive tampering with plaintiff's incoming and outgoing correspondence.

15. Defendant Panzer was notified of the mail tampering issue via a carbon copy of a letter sent to the trial judge on October 9, 1974.

16. Defendant Panzer neither filed any motion objecting to such

conduct by the FBI nor informed the plaintiff that such actions constituted Fourth Amendment violations.

17. Defendant Panzer talked to the plaintiff only once before trial, informed him his fingerprints were all over the evidence (a lie), and attempted to coerce the plaintiff into an insanity defense.

18. Defendant Panzer refused to communicate with the plaintiff before trial, made no attempt to prepare any type of defense, and as a result the plaintiff's mother was forced to hire defendant Hanes. Defendant Hanes paid defendant Panzer a substantial sum to assist in the plaintiff's defense and defendant Panzer then "called in sick" the day of the trial and did nothing further for the defendant.

19. Defendant Hanes also refused to raise the Fourth Amendment issue, mail tampering, with the trial court either before, during, or after trial though he had knowledge of it.

20. Defendant Salten was negligent in the handling of plaintiff's case in that when she transferred the plaintiff's transcript of trial she "neglected" to enclose the plaintiff's pre-trial motion and correspondence.

21. Defendants Young and Bamberger were negligent in (1) their procurement of the plaintiff's <u>complete</u> trial and pre-trial proceedings and (2) in their willful failure to communicate with the plaintiff before they submitted an appeal brief on his case. Evidently, neither of them were aware of the plaintiff's pre-trial motion or deliberately bypassed them.

22. As a result of the defendants' combined negligence, the District Court of the Southern District of New York denied a 28 USC 2255 proceeding April 22, 1977 deeming the issue had been "deliberately bypassed" and "waived" and the Second Circuit Court of Appeals affirmed that decision on November 2, 1977.

23. Such "bypass" and waiver was solely the fault of the defendants as the plaintiff had no formal training in law, was not aware of 18 USC 1701 and 1702 until September of 1976 while the 2255 petition was being prepared and was unaware that such conduct constituted a "fourth amendment" violation until it was pointed out by the U.S. Attorney in the response to that 2255 petition.

SAMPLE DOCUMENT

V. LEGAL CLAIMS

24. The four elements of negligence are present in the instant case:

A. A duty, or obligation, recognized by the law, requiring the actor to conform to a certain standard of conduct, for the protection of others against unreasonable risks.

B. A failure on their part to conform to the standard required.

C. A reasonable close causal connection between the conduct and the resulting injury.

D. Actual loss or damage resulting to the interests of another.

25. The four elements of legal malpractice are also present:

A. Contract for professional service.

B. Reliance by plaintiff.

C. Failure to exercise professional skill.

D. Damage caused by that failure.

26. The plaintiff, unable to litigate and/or vindicate a Constitutional right because of the negligent conduct of the defendants, in addition to the extra time he has spent in prison, must live in fear of being "violated" on parole until September 10, 1979 and spend the rest of his life deprived of his rights under the Second Amendment, the right to own firearms.

RELIEF REQUESTED

1. Compensatory damages in the amount of $50,000 from each defendant.

2. Punitive damages in the amount of $50,000 from each defendant.

3. Trial by jury on all issues triable by jury in accordance with the provision of Federal Rule of Civil Procedure 38(a) and (b).

4. Plaintiff's cost of this action.

5. Such other relief as this Court deems just, proper, and equitable.

NOTARY PUBLIC

Brenda S. Carl

MY COMMISSION EXPIRES:

JUNE 14, 1980

RESPECTFULLY SUBMITTED,

Michael H. Brown

MICHAEL H. BROWN

101 CHERRY RD.

BEREA, KENTUCKY 40403

SAMPLE DOCUMENT

UNITED STATES DISTRICT COURT
SOUTHERN DISTRICT OF INDIANA
TERRE HAUTE DIVISION

MICHAEL H. BROWN and HAROLD JAMES JENKS, Plaintiffs, -vs- KATHERINE LOUDERMILK, J. B. JOHNSON and J. W. JEAN, Defendants.	)	NO. TH 78-117-C

E N T R Y

This cause came before the Court on the Complaint of Plaintiffs and Defendants' Motion to Dismiss. The Court having examined said Complaint and Motion to Dismiss now finds that the said Motion to Dismiss should be sustained.

IT IS THEREFORE ORDERED that the Motion of the Defendants to dismiss Plaintiffs' Complaint is hereby SUSTAINED and this cause is hereby DISMISSED.

s/ James E. Noland
JAMES E. NOLAND, Judge
United States District Court

Dated: Oct 17, 1978

Memorandum

This Complaint was originally filed in the Eastern District of Kentucky where summons was ordered issued. Defendants, by Assistant United States Attorney,

Appendix E

for said district, filed their Motion to Dismiss or in the Alternative to Transfer the cause to the Southern District of Indiana, which transfer was granted.

In the Complaint, Plaintiffs allege that it is for declaratory relief and damages because of Defendants' collective and deliberate interference with Plaintiffs' rights of access to the Courts. Although Plaintiffs allege that Plaintiff Brown has a legal residence in Berea, Kentucky, they do not state the location of Plaintiff Jenks. Basically, Plaimtiffs allege that Defendants conspired to deny Plaintiffs access to the Courts by refusing to file a "next friend" habeas corpus petition submitted by Brown on behalf of Jenks. Plaintiffs identify said petition for habeas corpus as TH 76-88-C. They further allege that due to Defendant Loudermilk's refusal, Plaintiff Brown did not receive a hearing on the habeas corpus petition from June 15 to November 23, 1976. Petitioners further allege that Defendant Loudermilk interferred with Brown's civil rights by unauthorized disclosure of information, that Loudermilk unlawfully caused the ruling on habeas corpus petition to be sent to wrong address and caused Brown to be threatened with disciplinary action by Defendant Jean if Brown wrote any more letters to Loudermilk. Plaintiffs pray for declaratory judgment, compensatory and punitive damages, costs and an order removing each defendant from government employment.

On July 14, 1978, the Assistant United States Attorney for the Southern District of Indiana filed an answer in admission and denial and that the Defendants as federal officers are immuned from liability for actions taken in good faith within the scope of their duties.

SAMPLE DOCUMENT

Plaintiffs' complaint fails to state a claim against Defendant Jean as the only reference to him is contained in paragraph 11, wherein Plaintiffs allege Jean and Johnson at the time "of the foregoing instance" were both Plaintiffs' caseworkers. The "foregoing instance" refers to alleged threat attributed to Johnson concerning further letters to Loudermilk. Plaintiffs' complaint fails to state a claim against Defendant Johnson as the allegation concerning the threat contributed to him is conclusory only and further does not rise to a constitutional level. The Plaintiffs' allegations concerning the Defendants conspiring to deny Plaintiffs access to the Courts is unsupported and conclusory only as to Jean and Johnson and contain no facts that any conspiracy existed or could be implied between them or with Loudermilk.

As to the alleged claim against Loudermilk, the record clearly shows that the alleged action or inaction by Loudermilk regarding the Petition for Habeas Corpus in TH 76-88-C, was within her capacity as Deputy Clerk of this Court. Indeed the exhibits attached to Petitioners' complaint evidence this fact. The other records of this Court show the legal reasons for the alleged delay complained of. While acting within her capacity as an officer of this Court, Loudermilk is immuned from suit. Even without immunity, there is not sufficient claim for which Loudermilk could be subject to any suit. The allegation that Loudermilk unlawfully caused the ruling on the habeas corpus petition to be sent to the wrong address fails to state a claim. Plaintiffs' claim that she caused Brown to be threatened by Jean with disciplinary action is completely unfounded and a conclusion and therefore fails to state a claim.

Appendix B

Miscellaneous

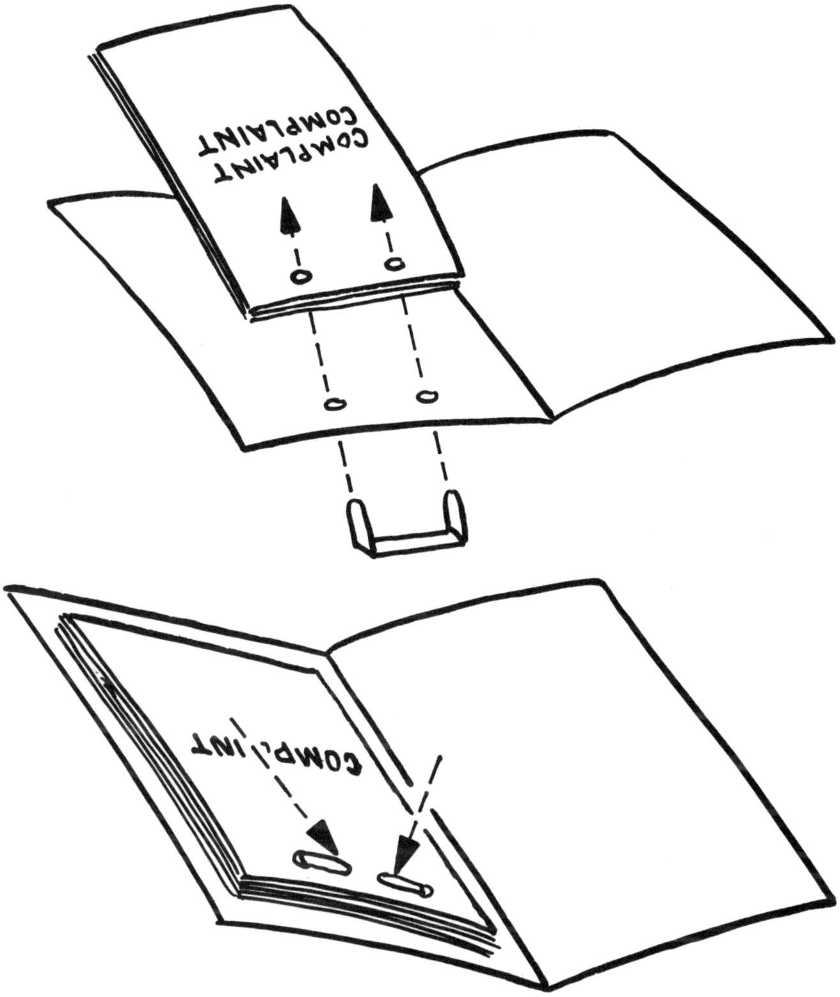

When keeping track of a civil action use a manila folder and bend-over metal tabs in the manner shown. Put the complaint in first, numbered front to back; then the answer and counterclaim on top, your answer on top of that, and so on. This allows you to flip to the most recent paperwork without digging through already plowed ground. Also makes adding to the stack easier.

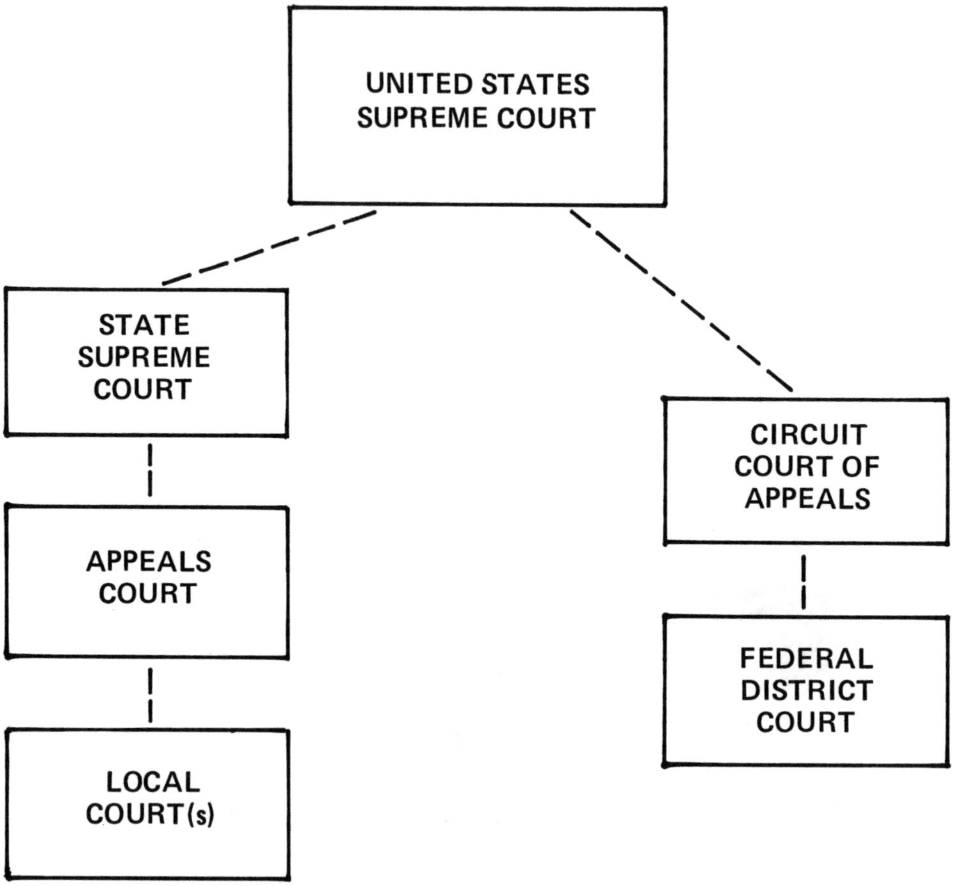

The United States Supreme Court is not the "final authority" – Congress is. The present Supreme Court is so far out in left field that Congress has to drag it back to center about once every 90 days by passing laws to over-rule their erroneous decisions. One of the more famous cases they mismanaged was STONE v POWELL – in which they declared 28 USC 2254 (federal habeas corpus for state prisoners) "null and void" because "the courts were overcrowded".

STONE v POWELL received a full page in Playboy several years back. Hugh Hefner didn't like it either.

THE NATIONAL LAW JOURNAL Monday, January 26, 1981

Studying Law as a Science

A 50-YEAR-OLD political science professor from Michigan State University says he's attending the University of Michigan Law School so he can do consulting work for attorneys who try cases before the U.S. Supreme Court.

Harold J. Spaeth says he decided to go to law school after nearly 20 years of using computer analyses to predict the outcome of Supreme Court cases.

Mr. Spaeth, who believes the personal attitudes of judges influence their decisions far more than do legal theories, specializes in looking at the voting records of the Supreme Court justices. His predictions have reportedly been 93 percent correct during the past seven years.

"My approach makes me something of an iconoclast in the legal profession," said Mr. Spaeth, who expects his Juris Doctor in December. "My empirical data show that the touted reliance of the legal profession on rational theory is pure myth." Mr. Spaeth said justices usually pick the precedents and legal theories that will support the conclusions they wish to uphold. These legal theories, he said, serve to mask the underlying attitudes of the judges.

Hermansdorfer to Resign From Bench; Was Criticized for His Coal Interests

Herald East Kentucky Bureau

U.S. District Judge H. David Hermansdorfer of Ashland, who was often criticized because of his coal interests, is resigning from the federal bench, effective Feb. 1.

In a resignation letter to President Carter, Hermansdorfer said that his last day in court will be Jan. 31.

Hermansdorfer, 49, has not heard any cases since last month, when he underwent surgery for a slipped disc at Cleveland Clinic in Ohio. He had been bothered by a painful back problem for more than a year.

In November 1979, Hermansdorfer announced his attention to resign, but did not step down because of the illness of Judge Bernard T. Moynahan Jr., who suffered a heart attack.

"The combination of events makes this a good time to resign, since Judge Moynahan has recovered and is back at work," he told the Ashland Daily Independent last week.

He said last week that since submitting his resignation he has been negotiating with a large Kentucky law firm for a job advising its clients on matters involving federal litigation. Hermansdorfer could not be reached for comment last night.

Hermansdorfer was appointed to the bench by President Nixon in 1972. Some critics later implied that Hermansdorfer's hearing of cases involving the coal industry amounted to a conflict of interest because of his financial interest in coal.

The American Lawyer, a legal journal, last year called him the worst judge in the U.S. 6th Circuit Court District, saying the "clincher" was his "biased view in favor of coal operators."

"In another district, Hermansdorfer's bias might be unimportant, but in the Eastern District of Kentucky, where much of the nation's coal mining goes on, Hermansdorfer's pro-management outlook is crucial to any evaluation of his performance," the legal journal said.

Hermansdorfer was one of six men recommended for a seat on the U.S. Court of Appeals for the 6th Circuit, but the vacancy went to Boyce Martin, then chief judge of the Kentucky Court of Appeals.

From the Lexington (KY) *Herald*, January 17, 1981

Index

Notes